ambulance + girl

By Jane and Michael Stern

AMAZING AMERICA

AMERICAN GOURMET

CHILI NATION

DOG EAT DOG

EAT YOUR WAY ACROSS THE U.S.A.

THE ENCYCLOPEDIA OF BAD TASTE

ELVIS WORLD

HAPPY TRAILS

JANE & MICHAEL STERN'S ENCYCLOPEDIA OF POP CULTURE

REAL AMERICAN FOOD

ROADFOOD

SIXTIES PEOPLE

SQUARE MEALS

TRUCKER

TWO PUPPIES

WAY OUT WEST

HOW I
SAVED MYSELF BY BECOMING
AN EMT

Jane Stern

ambulance girl

THREE RIVERS PRESS • NEW YORK

Some of the names, locations, and details of events in this book have been changed to protect the privacy of persons involved.

Published by Three Rivers Press, New York, New York.
Member of the Crown Publishing Group, a division of Random House, Inc.
www.crownpublishing.com

THREE RIVERS PRESS is a trademark and the Three Rivers Press colophon is a registered trademark of Random House, Inc.

Originally published in hardcover by Crown Publishers, a division of Random House, Inc., New York in 2003

Printed in the United States of America

DESIGN BY ELINA D. NUDELMAN

Library of Congress Cataloging-in-Publication Data
Stern, Jane.
Ambulance girl : how I saved myself by becoming an EMT / by Jane Stern.
p. cm.
1. Stern, Jane. 2. Emergency medical technicians—Connecticut—Biography. I. Title.
RA645.6.C8 S747 2003
616.02'5'092—dc21

2002014762

ISBN 1-4000-4869-9

10 9 8 7 6 5 4 3 2 1

First Paperback Edition

TO MICHAEL STERN FOR SO MANY YEARS
OF LOVE AND INSPIRATION

AND FOR THOMAS E. KNOX, M.D., WHO SHOWED ME
THE WAY OUT OF THE DARKNESS

acknowledgments

Although this book has only my name on it, I need to acknowledge my husband, Michael Stern, for the constant support and endless help he provided me. I would also like to express my heartfelt gratitude to my agent, attorney, and longtime friend, Michael I. Rudell, for believing in *Ambulance Girl* and finding a good home for it. That happy place was with my editor, Annik La Farge at Crown Publishers, who guided my hand and heart to get the story right. Dorianne Steele at Crown was a pleasure to work with and made the publishing process a delight. I would also like to thank Neil J. Rosini at Franklin, Weinrib, Rudell & Vassallo for his insightful advice, as well as Bill Adams at Crown, who also read the manuscript with a keen eye. Special thanks to Allison J. Bloom, my attorney in Connecticut, who as a veteran EMT gave me not only exceptional legal advice but saved me from embarrassment with any technical writerly blunders. This book could not have been completed without hand-holding by my dear friends Bunny Kyle and Joanne Driscoll, who saw me through the hard parts. Thank you one and all.

1

I am G-65.

That is the number I was given when I became an Emergency Medical Technician at the volunteer fire company in Georgetown, Connecticut. I live in Georgetown, a rural, blue-collar town whose main attraction is a sprawling defunct wire mill with broken windows.

If you live in Georgetown and press 911, the dispatcher will tone me out. I will get on the two-way police radio in my car and say, "G-65 EMT responding."

I have another name, too: *Ambulance Girl* . . . as in, "Honey, the ambulance girl is here." I hear this as I drag myself, my portable oxygen tank, my defibrillator, and a giant bag of medical supplies into the homes of sick strangers.

I wait for my tone twenty-four hours a day, seven days a week. It comes over any of my three police radios: upstairs and downstairs at home, and in my car. My tone goes like this: two long beeps (one higher than the other), followed by five short beeps. It pulls me out of deep sleep, out of showers, away from the dinner table, from my favorite TV shows, away from arguing with my husband, away from phone calls telling me I owe money to the department store, and away from long, slow, loving embraces. I could pretend I didn't hear the tone but I don't. I would have nightmares about the people I left alone and suffering.

I am an EMT-B. This places me smack in the middle of the emergency care hierarchy. The top EMTs are the paramedics. They are full-time professionals who can insert airways that will allow you to breathe, place syringes into your chest cavity if your lungs collapse, or start an IV in your arm filled with enough morphine to make the bone-jarring ride to the hospital feel like you are a baby in its mother's arms. Some paramedics wear paramilitary uniforms and people refer to them in awe as paragods because they appear to be a cross between emergency room physicians and Green Berets.

To become an EMT-B I had to take a difficult course, pass state and national boards, work hours in the hospital emergency room, and keep my skills polished enough to recertify every few years. Although I am a volunteer at my fire department, and receive no salary, my training is the same as the paid professionals'.

As an EMT-B I can help you administer your own nitroglycerin if you are having a heart attack, shoot you in the thigh with a syringe of epinephrine if you are in anaphylactic shock, and stick a plastic airway into your throat and pump air into your lungs if you stop breathing. I can zap you back to life with a defibrillator if your heart stops. I can help you give birth to your baby in the back of the ambulance.

On the job I don't look like much. My favorite uniform is a used blue gabardine jacket with a brown corduroy collar that says GEORGETOWN EMS across the back in light-reflective two-inch letters. By the time I got it, its previous owners had lost the thermal liner, and so it is as limp as a Kleenex from years of wear. In the winter the wind whips through it; in the summer it sags from humidity. There are bleach and disinfectant stains on it from EMTs who wore this jacket before me and who tried to remove the effluvium of various sick people, drunks, women in labor, and the nearly dead who regularly ride with us in the back of our ambulance.

Many EMTs at level B look sharp. But they don't work for my town. They work in the surrounding wealthier towns of Fairfield County, Connecticut—towns such as Westport and New Canaan. These EMTs work on assigned shifts and wear crisp uniforms and sport important-looking gold badges. Their ambulances are replaced every few years from their towns' big budgets. Our ambulance is old, its interior is avocado green Naugahyde, the shag rugs in the driver's compartment thin with age. Our ambulance sputters and lurches and drips green fluid from its underbelly. When we pull up to the hospital and park it alongside the fancy ambulances, the security staff knows us on sight. They look at us like we are the Beverly Hillbillies arriving in the rattle-ass truck with Granny sitting on top in her rocker.

I took my EMT training in the posh town of New Canaan, where the ambulance cot blankets look like the monogrammed coverings of show horses. In short time I noted that our instructors had two ways of explaining how to remedy any situation. "In New Canaan we would use this stretcher strap or cravat, but for those of you who will be in service in other towns [glance toward me] you can always use duct tape instead." In my imagination, if our ambulance service had a heraldic crest, it would be a roll of duct tape on a field of spilled oil. Duct tape (which I confess I have never once seen used in my time as a Georgetown EMT) became the operative semantic symbol of the dividing line between Fairfield County snooty and Fairfield County down-to-earth.

When I became an EMT my friends were confounded. In fact, they thought it was ridiculous. They knew me to be a woman deeply and neurotically terrified of sick and dead people, a raging former urban Jewish hypochondriac on the order of Woody Allen, a sufferer from motion sickness in moving vehicles who always threatened to vomit if I was not allowed the front seat. I was someone who loved my sleep and privacy and tried never to go out in public without looking well-groomed.

But the closest I have ever felt to God is in the back of my ambulance. The most fully alive I have felt was when I held a dead man's head wedged between my knees and ventilated him back to life. One of the most precious moments of my life was the night I connected with a dying crack addict with AIDS who shared the same taste in gospel music as I do.

In my real life I am a writer for *Gourmet* magazine, but I am in bliss after a hard call when my coworkers and I pull the ambulance up to Dunkin' Donuts and share greasy crullers and a big cup of stomach-churning coffee and vent out all the stress to each other.

This is my story, about life and death, fear and joy, good and evil as seen from the back of an ambulance in a small town in Connecticut. Although it is my experience, it is also about all the rescue workers who will save your life if you call 911. None of us is unique. We are the people who know the secrets behind the closed doors on every street in town, and we are there to protect you from harm when you call.

What is different about my story is that in helping others I learned to help myself. Becoming part of a firehouse and working side by side with the men and women of the Georgetown Volunteer Fire Department saved me from a spiral into depression and middle-age angst. It was the hardest and the most rewarding task I ever set for myself. In doing so I found a family within the town I lived in, and learned that I could face what scared me in life. That is the story I will tell in this book.

2

My hometown has its own zip code and its own phone prefix, but it is not really a town in the normal scheme of things. Instead it is a patchwork quilt of a place. In addition to a small hunk of land called Georgetown it is made up of scraps and end pieces of the bigger and wealthier towns that surround it. It includes pieces of Redding and Wilton, a bit of Ridgefield and Weston, too. Georgetown is about an hour and twenty minutes from New York City but feels light-years away. One of our volunteer company fire trucks has THE HUB OF FAIRFIELD COUNTY painted on it, but Georgetown is only hub-like in that people roar through it on the way to someplace else. Not much happens in Georgetown, at least for the casual observer to see.

The Georgetown Volunteer Fire Company is situated across the street from the defunct Gilbert and Bennett wire mill that remains the centerpiece of the town. Once a thriving seat of industry when it began producing wire insect screening in 1861, then went on to manufacture meat and cheese safes, coal screens, and ox muzzles, it is now a crumbling castle of neglect. The huge ghostly building has been unoccupied for years; its windows are mostly all smashed in.

There are always town plans to *do something* with the property, to turn it into a spiffy housing community, loft spaces for artists, or a block of boutiques; but despite the creative ideas and slews of potential investors, the factory still sits abandoned.

When my husband, Michael, and I moved to the Redding part of Georgetown in 1982, we came from Weston, a mere five miles away. It was like coming to another country. Weston was the classic rich man's commuting town. Movie stars and CEOs lived there. The town center was a modest island of upmarket stores. The drugstore sold scented French candles and coffee table books about sailing. The main street of Georgetown was remarkable for its utter lack of yuppie charms. When we moved here, the main street had many liquor stores, a TV repair store that threw the nonfixable sets out on the pavement, and an old-fashioned barbershop whose owner probably had never heard of Frederick Fekkai.

While the surrounding towns are a source of endless magazine and local newspaper articles about their well-protected wildlife, scenic roads, and artistic residents, news from Georgetown seems to revolve around public sewers that are always backing up into local businesses and the fate of the defunct wire factory that sits like a toad in the middle of town. Georgetown was the town that the commuter train to New York whizzed past, shaking the down-at-the-heels houses on both sides of the tracks.

Technically Michael and I live in West Redding, but we are so close to Georgetown, that is where our fire tax goes, and that is the fire department that comes if we call 911. We moved from Weston to West Redding because we wanted to be in a more rural area. Weston was too expensive for us to move to a bigger and nicer house, while the Georgetown end of West Redding was still affordable. Weston had become a commuter town while West Redding, ten minutes farther from New York City by Metro-North, the commuter train, still had a country air about it. Even though Georgetown center was a stone's throw from our house, we disengaged ourselves from it emotionally when we bought a cheerful yellow colonial house high on a hill in West Redding. We hoped that when friends came to visit they would not notice the ugly old mill and the dreary main street of Georgetown, but would spring back to consciousness when, a mile up the road, where we lived on Wayside Lane, everything became leafy and bucolic again.

For years I passed the Georgetown Volunteer Fire Company on the way to the post office or the bank. I knew it was there but it never intrigued me. It had no sense of mystery about it the way the old wire mill did or the houses by the railroad tracks. The firehouse is a mundane redbrick building with a flagpole that flies an American flag and a second flag commemorating POWs and MIAs. Occasionally I would see the fire trucks lined up outside or see the ambulance zooming out of its parking bay. I never paid much attention; it was just part of the local landscape.

I had called 911 only one time since moving to Georgetown. I called to rat out a neighbor whose property borders mine, who liked to burn huge amounts of brush in bonfires so large that they threatened to leap across the property line and set my house on fire. I hid when I heard the fire trucks coming, to make sure the man didn't know I had turned him in, and I peeked out from the second-floor window to see the firemen extinguishing the blaze and watch the pantomime of the men lecturing my neighbor not to do it again. I was never a fan of emergencies of any nature. If there was an accident on the highway, I tucked my head in my hands and didn't look. I feared death and disfigurement. I did not want to see pain or blood or broken glass.

Outside the Georgetown Volunteer Fire Company was placed the kind of sign that you stick magnetic letters on, like a deli or a church has. The sign was always there. It said:

VOLS. WANTED . . . *FIRE EMS*

Sometimes, if the wind had blown off a few letters it read VO S WANT D. It too was just part of the scenery. I was fifty-two years old. I was not going to be a fireman.

But there was something about the EMS part of the sign that stuck in my mind. It pointed me to everything cowardly I knew about myself, about my fear of death and disease, my claustrophobia about being in moving vehicles that I am not driving. I was so suggestible about illness that I never watched the popular hospital shows like *ER*. I was not an EMT groupie, but something about the sign would not leave my mind.

Looking back, to do something that went against the way I defined myself should not have seemed so surprising. I was having a midlife "event," if not a full-blown crisis. This event entailed trying to think about ways I could make my life less miserable.

I was miserable. In fact, I was clinically depressed. I had spent my whole life paralyzed by my fears. Fearfulness and general nutty behavior was a family legacy. I had a grandmother who was so agoraphobic that she did not leave her house for thirty years; I had a father who had a dozen tics and suffered from obsessive-compulsive disorder, as well as from the consequences of having a steel plate surgically implanted in his skull from a horrendous head-trauma accident he suffered as a child. He flew into fits and rages at the slightest provocation. Just about everyone in my family was odd in some way. Despite becoming successful professionals, my aunts, uncles, and cousins wouldn't fly, wouldn't take boats, wouldn't use public phones, wouldn't eat in restaurants for fear of being poisoned. My most notorious relative (about whom I know very little) was apparently one of the original celebrity stalkers. Even though it was spoken about only in hushed tones when I was a kid, it was clear that a second cousin on my mother's side lived out his days at Pilgrim State Hospital for the Insane after being removed from a White House bedroom where he was caught looking for Harry Truman's daughter while wearing a woman's mink coat.

At age fifty-two, my own longtime teetering toward depression had caught up with me. I spent my days walking around the house in a baggy blue bathrobe. It was hard to find the energy to get dressed, and, quite frankly, there was no pressing need. As a writer, I worked at home. Days could go by when I would not see anyone but my husband, Michael. I could talk on the phone but people could not see what I looked like. We had no kids to attend to. The dog didn't care that I looked like shit. It was hard to find the incentive to run a comb through my hair, to brush my teeth. The bed went unmade. I spent hours sitting in my favorite chair, a green leather recliner, watching TV. I knew by heart the timetable for Ricki Lake, Oprah, and Sally. I sat, I ate, and I watched TV. My pants grew tight and I didn't care. Michael and I had started to drift apart. After more than thirty years of marriage and a long career together it seemed that he had blossomed and I had wilted on the vine. He was active and trim, riding his horse daily, having coffee with a close group of friends, while I sat in my bathrobe looking at shows like "My Wild Teen Wants to Have a Baby." I hated myself, and the spiral of depression fed by self-loathing exacerbated the growing chasm between us.

I was able to pull myself together for the occasional business meeting or lunch in New York with an editor, but my days at home were long and empty and sad. I didn't want to talk to anyone. Friends started to slip away. I didn't return phone calls; I let letters pile up on my desk. Who had the energy to engage with people? Not I. The highlight of my day was a drive out to the supermarket for magazines and cookies. Once I looked down and realized I was wearing my bedroom slippers instead of shoes.

I used to like to have people over for dinner. Now the mahogany dining table we had worked so hard to afford sat covered with a layer of dust. Candles that I had lovingly placed in silver holders sagged and I left them unstraightened. I went to the local library and took out books. I was looking at one on depression when the librarian came up to me and said, "I haven't seen you in a while. What are you working on?"

I was mortified. I was working on getting out of bed, which took hours. I don't think she wanted to hear this. "Oh, some great new projects," I lied; and she walked away with a chipper it's-always-great-to-see-local-authors smile. I put the library on my rapidly growing avoidance list. People knew me there and I would have to pretend to be normal.

I dreaded going out of the house. I could hardly drive my car anymore without panic and anxiety taking over.

If I had been a drinker I would have self-medicated and become a drunk. Instead I ate cookies and my pants got snugger. I signed up for the gym, lasted through one session, and never went back.

The anxiety was possibly worse than the depression. At least the depression had me in bed each day at one in the afternoon for my three-hour nap, exhausted from a morning of watching TV and doing nothing. "Don't you want to go to the barn with me and see the horses?" Michael asked.

I knew my horse was going unridden, and probably felt abandoned. "Maybe tomorrow," I said, and drifted off to the sweet sleep of temporary oblivion. Riding seemed an impossibility. Sometimes I would go to the closet in the bathroom where I kept the manicure utensils and nail polishes and look at them, I would pick out a polish and go back to sitting in my chair. I looked down and my feet seemed too far away to deal with, too much effort, too great a stretch.

Michael and I were working on weekly segments for a show to which we contributed on National Public Radio. We would broadcast each week sounding like we had the greatest job in the world: chipper, the world's most loving couple, the happiest people on earth. Our producer called and told us that radio listeners wanted to meet us, and we were to fly to Minneapolis, where the radio station had arranged a bus trip with our fans to a restaurant about three hours into the country.

I wondered if I could do all this. First I had to pull myself together and pack for the trip. I had to look decent; I could not meet National Public Radio listeners in my blue bathrobe. Then Michael and I had to take a plane trip, something we had done often but that I always dreaded. Fear of flying was high on my list of discomforts. And then, once we landed, I had to do the most heinous thing of all: ride on a bus. It had been thirty-five years since I'd set foot on one. I was totally phobic about buses. I hated public transportation, refused to take it, and now three hours with a group of strangers on a bus going who-knows-where . . . well, it was not something I looked forward to.

The producer of our show, Sally Swift, is a wonderful person—smart, funny, and sympathetic; so I got up the nerve to be candid with her. "I don't do buses," I said. I felt like a diva; in fact I was a depressed mess. After about twenty minutes of explanation, we agreed that Michael would ride the bus and I would follow behind the bus in Sally's car.

"I'll try to get on the bus, maybe it will work," I said to Michael. On the flight to Minneapolis I practiced thinking about a bus, and then getting on it. I visualized what a bus looked like. The only buses I rode were the ones from the airport to the car rental place and I hyperventilated the whole time. Being a passenger put me out of control, and all my anxiety stemmed from a fear of forfeiting or losing control. If I couldn't drive the bus or have Michael drive it, it was unbearable. The more I knew that someone else controlled the opening or closing of the bus doors, the higher my anxiety level went. To me, the air in the airport bus was stale and sickening, and the level of noise from people making happy conversation became shrieking and painful to my ears.

The night before the bus ride we went to Sally's house for dinner. I wanted to cry. I wanted her life. She was thin and athletic and pregnant with her second baby. Her first child was gorgeous and sweet and the house she and her husband, Tom, lived in was perfect. Every object was aesthetically lovely, her garden bright and blooming with herbs and flowers, the food she served a bounty of homegrown vegetables and delicious homemade breads. It was also perfectly casual; Sally wore her trademark bright red sneakers and seemed to host the dinner party effortlessly. I wanted her life—but what the hell would I do with it? The flowers and fruits would all wilt and rot as I sat in my green chair and watched the *Ricki Lake Show.* I was nauseous from the good health and calm that radiated from this happy household.

But the next morning I managed to pull myself together enough to resemble the bright chatty person people heard on the radio. These listeners were paying a hundred bucks apiece to meet Michael and me, so I felt it was the least I could do to wash my face. When Michael and I got to the bus in which we were going to spend the next six hours, I panicked. It looked like a car-rental bus and I didn't like the driver's looks. He looked like the type of person who would not stop the bus if I asked him to.

"I can't do this," I whispered to Michael. I could see the look of frustration on his face. "I'm sorry," I said, wishing I could give him money or a gift to make up for my shortcomings as a wife and partner.

"I can't do this," I said to Sally, who was blessedly cool about it.

"Yeah, you said you would rather ride in the car with me," she said.

I felt like a big baby. I thought about all the field trips in grade school that I missed because I was afraid to be on a bus, or away from home. My phobias and separation anxieties went way back to my childhood. "I'll talk to the listeners when we get to the restaurant," I said, trying to make it better. I felt like an asshole as I got in the front seat of her car.

At the end of a long day, the bus trip was over. Michael had been charming enough for both of us; our listeners seemed happy. They liked the NPR tote bags that were given to them and they had liked the restaurant we had traveled so many miles to eat at.

I was glad, but I was still complaining. "I don't know why we couldn't have just eaten somewhere in Minneapolis," I said to Michael as we sat waiting for the plane. "There are plenty of great places to eat there."

Michael looked at me. I could tell he was tired and pissed off. "They live in Minneapolis. The point was to go on an adventure, go somewhere new," he said.

I got defensive. "I think it is stupid. There are many good places to eat in town that we wouldn't have to take a bus to." Michael chose not to answer. He took out his laptop computer and started to work, staring at the small screen so he could block me out.

We were not going home. We were headed for Chicago, a fifty-five-minute flight from Minneapolis. We had been asked to give a lecture the next day at a Chicago-based think tank. They wanted to know what we had observed about other people's eating habits: what they ate, what aisles they shopped in the supermarket, what food magazines appealed to what demographics. They were putting us up at the Four Seasons in a lavish suite and paying us well. It was exciting and I was looking forward to it.

With the long bus ride behind me, I never imagined that the true nightmare was just about to begin. We boarded the plane and taxied away from the gate. Then a strange thing happened. We headed off the main runway onto a smaller one, then taxied all the way to the farthest outskirts of the airport. There the plane stopped and shut off its engines.

My fear of flying had little to do with crashing, and everything to do with claustrophobia. To me a plane was a sealed metal tube—an MRI machine with wings. If it was moving in the direction it was supposed to be going, I was all right; but any delay caused my anxiety level to hit 10 on a scale of 1 to 10. It was dusk and I could see through the dirty little windows of the plane that we were not even near the airport anymore. The fact that the engines were turned off was a dire sign. I held my breath. I tried not to hyperventilate. I grabbed Michael's hand; mine was cold as ice and sweaty at the same time. Michael gave me *the look*—the look that comes from thirty years of living with someone who has raging anxiety. It is a look that is both sympathetic and reassuring. It is one of the many reasons to love Michael.

Finally the pilot clicked on the intercom. "Well, ladies and gentlemen," he droned in that familiar flat, emotionless way (are they taught to talk that way at pilot school?) "seems like we are going to sit here for a little while. O'Hare seems to be having some traffic control problems. I will let you know when we are taking off."

We sat on the runway for six hours. During this time my body pumped so much adrenaline that I thought I was having a heart attack every five minutes. Michael said every soothing thing he could think of. After three hours into the delay I stretched out limply over his lap and let him stroke my head. "When are we going to move?" I whined at Michael as if he were a fortune-telling genie who held the secret answer. I got up and paced the aisles. I tried to breathe deeply, I tried not to breathe. I felt my temples throbbing and was convinced I was having a stroke.

I reached into my purse and lapped up the powdered remains of a decade-old Valium that I had been carting around for just such an occasion. The container was so old that the doctor's name had worn off. The flight attendants were not pleasant; obviously they were pissed off too. The pilot stopped giving us updates after the first two hours. The sun had set and I could see nothing out the plane's windows, no lights, nothing.

The air was stale, the lavatory toilet clogged after the second hour, there was no food on the plane since it was only supposed to be an hourlong flight.

The Valium was useless. Michael did the best he could. He opened his wallet and showed me pictures of our pets. He tried to talk about what we would eat in Chicago when we landed. Nothing could get my attention from the fact that the plane was not moving. I died the thousand deaths of a coward before the plane finally took off.

By the time we arrived at the hotel my nervous system was so overtaxed that I propped myself up on the reception desk like a drunk on a lamppost. Once in our room I dived under the bedcovers and fell into a dreamless sleep.

Somehow I got through the presentation the next day, but on the return flight home our plane was again delayed two hours. I had run out of adrenaline. My body felt numb, and I felt disconnected and unreal. When I got home I called a psychiatrist that a friend had recommended. He was supposed to be good.

Psychiatry was not new to me. It was the family business. My uncles were psychoanalysts, even though, despite being members of distinguished university faculties and respected Freudian institutes, they were too phobic to fly on planes. They were very old school about the treatment of phobias, which meant they believed in talking about "underlying issues." My favorite uncle was at Yale Medical School and I remember how proud he was to have patients who had been with him for decades.

My uncle would take an ocean liner to Europe when he had to go to a psychiatric convention abroad, and when his own father was on his deathbed in Los Angeles, he and my mother took a five-day train trip across the country rather then set foot on a plane. My grandfather died two days before they arrived.

When Michael and I were students in graduate school, my uncle, who was having his office redecorated, gave us his well-worn leather analyst's couch. I imagined that to press on it would let lose a stream of cries and wails. In bed at night sometimes I fantasized the living room filling with floating words, years of why his patients were miserable and stuck in their fears and fantasies. The words circled the ceiling, not going anywhere.

As comfortable as I was about seeing a shrink, I was also skeptical. Blah, blah, blah, and big monthly bills was what I imagined. It seemed like a dead-end road to me.

But nonetheless I appeared for my first session with the new psychiatrist and found that I liked him even before I saw him. I was comforted by the delicate orchid that he had growing in the waiting room, the collection of wooden walking sticks, and artwork that was many levels above the usual museum posters and such that shrinks use to decorate their waiting rooms. He greeted me and ushered me into his office. I had already told him on the phone about my six hours on the runway. With a sympathetic shake of his blond hair, he began the session by saying, "What a fucking nightmare."

Ahh, at last: a shrink I could relate to, who expressed my sentiments perfectly. Maybe he could pull me out of the muck of depression and make it seem safe to venture out in the world again. Convince me, I thought, as I looked around his office, that the world is not just waiting to trap me in buses, airplanes, and in my own black stupor in front of the TV set.

I think that good psychotherapy is like love or friendship. So much of it is indefinable chemistry between two people. I had seen three shrinks before and had not felt any improvement. When I was a student at Yale my father died and my fear of buses and airplanes expanded to include elevators and subways. Taking a bus was something my therapist and I had talked about in depth. One day en route to a session, my car broke down in New Haven. I did a marathon run to his office, arriving only ten minutes late. "Why didn't you take a bus?" he asked me blankly. I felt like I had been talking to a wall for a year.

My new shrink's name was Tom Knox. The fact that I could not afford his rates did nothing to sour me on wanting to see him. I knew I belonged on that couch facing him in his black leather chair. I liked everything about him, from the bottoms of his shoes that faced me as he put them up on the ottoman in front of his chair to the Bose radio in his waiting room.

In our first sessions together he tried to have me recall if there was one moment, even a fraction of a second, in the endless adrenaline bath of panic I had taken on that plane, when I didn't feel like the whole world was collapsing around me.

Yes, there was. At one point about three hours into the ordeal, a high school kid who was on the first leg of a charter flight to Switzerland with his classmates took ill. He hadn't eaten all day and was feeling dizzy.

"There is nothing to eat on this plane," the flight attendant told him curtly, and he looked pale and frightened.

I had a candy bar in my handbag. I pulled it out and walked to the seat where he sat with a few classmates huddled around him trying to give him moral support. I asked him if he would like the candy bar, suggesting it might make him feel more energized. He looked uncomfortable but he took it. He ate it, and in about ten minutes his cheeks were pink and he was laughing with his friends.

The crisis over, I began fretting again about myself, about being trapped in the plane, but that few minutes of being involved in helping someone else worked like the Valium should have, but didn't.

I began seeing Tom Knox once a week. I checked his credentials, all good: Johns Hopkins for medical school, New York Hospital/Cornell Medical Center for internship and residency. He believed in talking, but he also believed in drugs. He put me on an antidepressant and I felt significantly better almost at once. He gave me a new fresh supply of Valium and told me to take it when I needed it, that carrying it around in my handbag for a decade was not going to help get me through my fears. I trusted him. I trusted his gray sweater vest and the good smell of the leather chairs inside his office. Maybe there was hope for me after all.

3

"I think I want to be an EMT," I told Tom during a session. I was amazed that he did not laugh at me. He smiled and said it sounded interesting. At this point he knew me well enough to know that my family history was not only awash with nutcases, but also littered with the sick and dead, and that the mere mention of illness caused my heart to race and my temples to throb.

By the time I was twenty-five, both my parents had died from cancer. My favorite uncle, the shrink at Yale, followed suit soon after, as did his twenty-nine-year-old daughter, who died from breast cancer. My aunt died of Alzheimer's, my other cousin died at twenty-three in a car wreck. Even my dog died during that grim period. It had all left me with a bad case of hypochondria. Every twinge was a brain tumor, MS, or a stroke. Something awful was always about to happen to me.

I had been seeing Tom Knox for about two months when I stopped, after a shrink session, at the Georgetown firehouse to talk to someone about becoming an

EMT. It was a spur-of-the-moment decision and I was dressed to kill, not to cure. I wore a long, flowing, three-tiered silk skirt and a bright red Chinese silk jacket with a mandarin collar, blue custom-made cowboy boots with my initials on them in yellow, and long silver and turquoise earrings. Since the antidepressants had kicked in I was again getting dressed and using makeup. I thought I looked pretty good.

The man in charge of accepting EMT applications was in his seventies, hard-nosed and gruff. His name was Charlie. He looked at me and said, "Lady, I don't think this is for you," then went into a long soliloquy about vomit.

Vomit was his personal nemesis, the world's worst and most abhorrent thing. He looked at my silk outfit. "They'll vomit all over you," he said, trying to scare me. He did. I hated vomit too. In fact, vomit was high on my scale of things that made me panic. I was so afraid of vomiting myself that it never occurred to me that I might be the target of someone else's spew.

Then came a not very subtle remark about my age (old) and my weight (heavy). The bottom line, as he saw it, was that I was too old, too fat, and too fancy for the job.

His dismissal of me had a strange effect. I went home and cried and pouted and fumed, and raged about the unfairness of everyone and everything. I called Tom Knox and cried to him, and then I got pissed off and decided that nothing in the world could stop me from becoming an EMT.

Nothing except perhaps my own formidable demons.

Top of the demon list was my lifelong claustrophobia. I woke up in a cold sweat at 2 A.M. trying to recall what an ambulance looked like. I remembered that they seemed to have two parts, the driver's compartment and the "room" part where the sick person was put. Were there windows in the back? Did the doors open from the inside? Was there a way to get from the back part to the driver's part if you had to? Or were you trapped in the back end with the sick, possibly vomiting person, locked in and unable to escape?

I paced the bedroom, and at 8 A.M. I called the firehouse and again spoke to Charlie. "Can I come and look at the ambulance?" I asked.

There was a long pause. I don't think he wanted to see me again but he said I could look at it if I wanted.

Later that day I went back to the firehouse. I didn't dare tell him about my claustrophobia or fear of moving vehicles, certainly wouldn't tell him I was afraid of sick people. This time I wore jeans and a T-shirt. I opened the doors of the back of "the bus," as it was referred to, and crawled in. I didn't like what I saw one bit. It was like a shrunken emergency room, oxygen masks and suction tubes and bandages and splints and other vile icons of death and dying were crammed into a small space.

A small passage space allowed contact with the front compartment and the doors could be opened from the inside, and the little windows opened to let in fresh air. It was not a totally sealed space, but it still gave me the creeps.

I looked at Charlie's face. He was going through the motions, but obviously couldn't wait for me to leave.

"What is it you wanted to look at exactly?" he asked.

"Nothing really, I just have never been inside an ambulance," I said and tried to imagine if I could squeeze myself through the space from the back to the front if I was freaking out in the back.

"Thanks . . . I think I would really like to become an EMT."

I don't know if he or I looked more shocked when I said those words. We both stared at each other mutely.

He took me upstairs, where I filled out paperwork that would enroll me for the class that would begin in a month.

As much as I hated the ambulance, I instantly loved the firehouse. It looked perfectly comfortable in the most manly, blue-collar way. The main room had a big-screen TV turned to a NASCAR race, comfortable couches, a bar area with open boxes of beef jerky sticks, a soda machine that delivered cans of Pepsi for free, a big pool table with a Budweiser sign over it, a pinball game from the 1950s, and a wooden shuffleboard table game called Horseshoe that looked like it was from the 1930s.

It was GI-barracks neat. Old fire helmets were in a display case and patches from other friendly fire departments were stapled to a burlap-covered board. I wanted to sit on the big couches and eat beef jerky with the guys.

I signed the paperwork and went home.

* * *

I walked in the door that leads from the garage to the kitchen to find Michael boiling a pot of water for spaghetti.

"Hi," he said. "Where were you?"

"At the Georgetown firehouse," I said as I watched him slide his favorite imported pasta into the water. "Guess what?" I said. "I'm going to be an EMT."

Michael stirred the pasta in the pot and got a bemused look on his face, as if I had told him that I figured out Santa Claus really existed. I had seen this look before. I had seen it when I came home declaring that I was going to take up the bagpipes, and I had seen it when I said I was going to sign up for boxing lessons at a raunchy gym in nearby Danbury. It was the look of disbelief and of humoring me along.

"Cool," he replied. "When do you start?"

I felt myself flush with annoyance. He thought I was just spinning my wheels.

"I'm not kidding," I insisted.

"Did I say you were?" he said back. "What do you do as an EMT?" he asked.

"You pull dying people from car wrecks and that kind of thing," I muttered.

Michael raised an eye at me. "That's what you want to do?" he asked.

"Absolutely," I said, feeling weak in the knees.

What Michael didn't know was that I had started the process of becoming an emergency medic almost half a century before. I was the child who was always playing doctor. I even had a specialty: head transplants. The transplants were an innovative technique that involved my twin teddy bears, George and Soft Baby, and a pair of sharp scissors. The procedure was to cut their heads off at the neck and then switch them. George got Soft Baby's head and vice versa. It was an elaborate and time-consuming operation. First the severed heads were placed on a clean towel, then a threaded needle from my mother's sewing box was sterilized with Arpège perfume. Two lengths of brocade ribbon bought from the notions department at Bloomingdale's were cut to size and the bear's heads were laboriously sutured to each other's bodies using the ribbon at the new neckline. I had perfected the operation after doing it at least a dozen times, so it was a shame when one day I got careless and accidentally knocked George's severed head off the windowsill, and it lay in the courtyard of the fancy building on Fifth Avenue that abutted the townhouse in which I lived with my parents. No matter how I cried and pleaded, the doorman would not leave his post and retrieve my bear's head from the courtyard. Formidable in his large great coat and cap, he sent me packing. He did not understand this was a medical emergency . . . a 911 call.

I started my real EMT training course on a freezing winter's day in the lecture room of the New Canaan police station. The cops behind the bulletproof window glowered as I entered. There were no kind looks given to me or the other forty people in the class who followed me in. We may not have been perps but we were interlopers in the cops' sanctuary. Over the microphone and through the bulletproof glass we were told not to loiter in the lobby, not to talk to the police, not to park in the nearby spaces in the parking lot reserved for police cars . . . to generally get lost, sit down, and shut up.

I immediately got so nervous I lost one of my favorite earrings, dropped my eyeglasses and bent the frames, and spilled the contents of my purse on the floor. None of the students made eye contact with each other. Everyone looked grim and nervous. The majority of the class were young men, firefighters or police trainees looking for their EMT certification.

The class ran three hours. We were given the textbooks. I opened mine at random and saw a large color photo of a man with half his head missing and his brain pouring out like gray pudding. I turned the page. There was a photo of a partial amputation of a limb, the jagged white bone protruding from what looked like a steamship round of beef. I turned it again and there was someone with third-degree burns on his penis, his skin hanging like scarlet ribbons down his leg. I felt the latte I had brought to class from the nearby Starbuck's roaring in the wrong direction up my gullet. Old, fat, and single-earringed, I prayed to not puke all over myself the first day. I tried to fade into the crowd.

Our instructor was a paramedic named Frank Posca. I

wanted Frank to like me but he made it clear he was not interested in friendship from anyone in the class. He was a tattooed ex-military man, a veteran of the streets of Bridgeport, where from the back of the ambulance he worked on a regular basis with crack addicts and glue sniffers and failed suicides. Frank was short and wide, a cinder block of a man with a closely barbered head and a tiny gold earring.

When I look now at the big white plastic loose-leaf notebook I carried to the class over the long months ahead, I see how neat and tidy my writing was in those first few classes. How I copied down in a firm black pen such nuggets of wisdom as "Professional attributes of an EMT are a neat clean appearance, current knowledge and skills, attention to patient care." I wondered if someone with their brain hanging out of their head would notice my "neat clean appearance" or my missing earring and bent eyeglasses.

Printed and in large letters in my notebook were Frank's words of warning that first day: "EMT is the most stressful job of all!" And below that, a list of the warning signs of stress, which included "anxiety, guilt, indecisiveness, isolation, fear of separation and being ignored." Since I already had all these symptoms before I set foot in the class, I wondered how I would know when the job was getting to me.

EMT training is like boot camp. This was a new way of learning to me. I was a product of exclusive Ivy League schools and progressive preps. My teachers were there to nurture me, to gently water the seed of my talents and coax it to the sunlight. The first day of class Frank had us all bellowing in unison the watchwords for becoming an EMT: "BSI . . . I'm number one!" we screamed.

BSI means Body Substance Isolation, i.e., protective gloves and, if necessary, a mask and eye protection and perhaps full fireman's turnout gear complete with self-contained breathing apparatus. If you are an EMT you do not go into a scene and you do not even think of touching patients without at least a barrier of rubber between you and them.

"I'm number one" means that you are important to yourself and to the rescue unit. If you arrive at the scene of an emergency and someone is pointing a gun at you, the house is burning down, toxic fumes are clouding the air, or a psychotic is telling you the Martians have ordered him to kill you now, you do not attempt to be a hero. You run for cover and get help. That is what being number one is all about.

When I left the first class I was so wrung out that my hands shook. I could hardly unlock my car door. As I drove home, it started to snow. I felt the car skid as I made the turns on the back roads. What if I had an accident and had to call 911? Could I tell them I was sort of one of them?

I got home shortly before midnight. It was late and Michael had gone to bed. I made myself a toasted bagel with cream cheese, sat downstairs in the den, and flipped the channel of the TV to an old Bette Davis movie. I thought of the gruesome pictures in the textbook and felt queasy again. I pushed the bagel aside, walked upstairs, and crawled into bed next to Michael, basking in his warmth. Safe for now.

The class met three times a week. Being back in a classroom flooded me with memories of childhood. I was now significantly bigger than the last time I sat at a school desk, and I now found the chair with the writing board that swung around under my right arm constrictive. I also had a lot more "stuff" than I did as a kid—a purse, a coffee mug—and I was minus a locker or cubbyhole in which to stash it.

I arrived chronically early to the class, scouted out my favorite chair on the far left of the front row, attractive to me because it was close to a window ledge where I could rest my stainless steel tankard of coffee, my handbag, and my textbooks.

Buying the notebook and pens for the class was a rush of nostalgia. I had not handled three-ring lined notebook paper in years. I bought a plastic pouch to hold pens and pencils, colorful plastic dividers to segregate one class neatly from another. I arrived freshly scrubbed, bright-eyed, and eager. I smiled at everyone who came in. Few returned my glance.

I was not the oldest person in the class. There were two people my senior. One was a small-boned woman, thin and jittery. The other was a man with a gray woolly head and thick glasses. My first thought when I looked at them was, They don't belong here. They were too old, too dilapidated. I smelled trouble; they would have special needs, be slow, be irritating. Ungenerous in my assessment, I wanted them out. I dreaded that anyone might think I was like them. Sure, I was more than thirty years older than most of my classmates, but it was obvious these people were really old and didn't belong here.

The jittery lady lasted one class. She fidgeted through the lecture and I saw her handing her textbook back to Frank at the end. I tried to make eye contact with her as she left the room but she held her head down.

The human body as I first learned about it as an EMT is a stick figure. That is what I drew in my notebook during the lecture. This stick man had lines going through him. Sideways he was cut into anterior and posterior segments, through the chest he was midclavicular, his twiglike fingers were distal to his medial section, his single line of a chest was proximal to his heart. The stick man's spine was divided into four sections. His cervical spinal process, his thoracic region, his lumbar region, and his sacral region. A big black ink splotch on his anterior thorax showed the xiphoid process, "landmark for all CPR compressions," we were told.

I loved the words of the body's geometry. They were poetry to me. *Scapula, maxilla, ischium, meniscus, calcaneus, acetabulum:* I moved them around in my mouth like smooth lapidary pebbles. I loved the word *cyanotic,* meaning blue from lack of oxygen. We saw slides. Dead was a gray blue like the churning waters off Gloucester, Massachusetts.

I was immediately good in class, but it was only because I knew the bones of the body from my years as an art student. Art was what I had majored in as an undergraduate as well as a grad student for seven academic years (about as long as it takes to become a medical doctor). I sketched and painted the human body. I came to know it draped and disrobed, fat and thin, young and old. I especially loved anatomy, loved tracing my hand across the ivory bones of the class skeleton, loved the books that showed the body dissected to reveal flaps of muscle and cartilage. Like architects building a house, as artists we had to learn what held this thing called the human body together. We had to know how it moved, and what lay under the skin.

I was strong coming out of the starting gate as an EMT. I had a leg up, I knew my tibia from my fibula. I hugged my white plastic loose-leaf to my chest as I left the class at the end of the night. I could do this. I knew things.

My jump start didn't last long. Was it possible that when I was younger and went to school five days a week that my brain could absorb as much information as I was getting now? Now I felt overwhelmed with facts. It was different than when I was a child. I remember classes and I remember homework, but this was unique. Maybe I cared more now, maybe my brain, like the rest of me, had slowed down. I wondered if the antidepressants were causing brain lock. I looked around the class and wondered if anyone else felt as overwhelmed and flooded as I did.

I think that I cared too much. I was the one who sat taking notes like mad. I was the one who always had my hand in the air. What Frank said to the class seemed like the wisdom on the tablets God gave to Moses.

Frank explains to us the correct placement of a plastic airway into the patient's throat. I can see myself ham-handed in the back of an ambulance, inserting the airway the wrong way. I cringe, and turn around to see the slack faces of my fellow classmates. They do not share my intensity, my horror of missing any of the minutiae. I see one of the two identical-looking Spanish sisters who have joined the class pushing her cuticles back. She is not listening. I am thinking, What if she was the EMT in an ambulance when I stopped breathing? What if someone handed her the plastic airway and she had not remembered that Frank had said something about putting it in one way and then flipping it around the opposite way during insertion? It ceases to matter, because after two more classes both sisters dropped out. I ran into them on the streets of the town two weeks later and asked them what happened. "Too gross," they say in unison. They didn't like the slides of people with their brains spilling out.

I am amazed I have stuck it out this far.

Frank is our main teacher but he is joined by five different paramedics from time to time who come in to lecture us. They seem to me to be a good ol' boys club. I think they regard us students as insignificant fleas skirling about on the surface of emergency medicine. During the breaks they ignore us and laugh and talk with each other.

Even though they hang together they all have different personalities. There is Ralph Miro, a trim, neatly dressed man who comes to lecture us wearing a well-cut suit and tie instead of the coplike uniform that Frank and the others must wear on the job. Despite his sartorial style he is the one who brings the most horrific slides to show us, and clearly delights in raising the squirm factor. He wants to scare away those who can't take it, or who think EMT is holding the hand of an attractive person with a hangnail and offering comfort and a bandage.

Ralph's photos are straight from the hospital and autopsy room. They are a gallery of freakish events. A man who fell on an iron fence railing that pierced his chest, a woman having an allergic reaction whose tongue has swollen to the size of a shoe. A man who was hit in the face straight on with a shotgun and whose nicely cut hairdo now frames what looks like a dish of eggplant parmesan. I am fascinated by what is left intact on these unfortunate people. We are supposed to be looking at a bloody stump of a wrist and I am seeing the grace of the hand that is left behind, the attractive nails and elegant ring on the good hand, the silky skin or the curve of a hip, the svelte fleece of pubic hair that glistens despite being a neighbor to disaster a few inches away.

I think I am weird to notice this, but I am looking for comfort in the midst of chaos. Maybe I am trying to remember these are people and not body parts. By the fourth class things have gotten so intense that I have taken to writing the name of my shrink in the well of my notebook over and over, in an attempt to keep from running out of the room.

I plead my case to the gods of medicine. "Let me get through this," I say. I think it can't be worse than sitting in the plane. I am listening to Prozac, but it hasn't told me everything will be all right.

The class is like a living and changing entity. Cliques form. There are now popular people and pariahs. During the breaks the same people talk with each other. The cops still give us dirty looks and yell at us about parking in their spots. The paramedics hang together, daring us to come near them, and I have made an uneasy alliance with a girl named Dot. At least a decade my junior, Dot wears her hair cut short, dyed purply red and spiked with gel.

Each of us takes our same seat each class. I hold on to the one near the window ledge with the force of a pioneer homesteader. I love this seat because the cracks of the window caulking leak just enough air to make me feel I will not pass out when the lecture gets too visceral. Dot has taken up residence in the seat next to mine. We are both front-row types—intense, educated, verbal. The difference between us is that she fails to understand that this is boot camp and the best way to survive is to be invisible. You don't want to piss off the paramedics. They clearly hate us just for being new and dumb and are looking for any excuse to make our class time more hellish. Somehow Dot doesn't get this, or if she does, she doesn't care, as she raises her hand every five minutes. She questions them, she argues with them, she corrects their grammar. I am wishing she was far away from me; I worry they will think I am in cahoots with her. "Shut up, shut up, shut up," I whisper under my breath. But she doesn't.

We are starting to get up from our desks and do what are called practicals. This involves Frank dividing the class into groups of six and practicing things like CPR or trauma assessments with each other instead of just sitting at our desks learning things theoretically. Dot is in a different group than I am. Frank has broken up the groups by last names rather than seat assignments.

I am having a wonderful time because I like the hands-on part. I now get to touch living people, my fellow students. Maybe it is my age or my training as an artist, but I am not at all shy about placing my hands on a stranger's body.

With the help of the paramedics we learn how to apply traction splints and cervical neck collars and how to cut off someone's clothing fast and look them over for bullet wounds that have entered and exited. We use each other and we use rubber mannequins to practice on. I am given a rubber baby doll and told to save it from choking. I do the pediatric Heimlich maneuver so hard the baby's head flies off and lands ten feet away in the corner of the room. This is not good.

I move on to the big adult-sized rubber mannequins. The female mannequin has blond plastic hair that looks like a 1950s swimming cap. All the mannequins' mouths gape open like sex dolls'. Many of them are just heads and torsos without arms or legs. These are for working on with chest compressions and mouth resuscitations. One mannequin, Rescue Randy, is dressed in real clothing and looks the most human. He is filled with sand and weighs 160 pounds, and is designed to duplicate an unconscious adult male. I tug at his legs to move him. He doesn't budge.

With the help of a classmate I haul Randy around the classroom, hitting his head on the desks and wooden baseboards. "You killed him!" Frank yells jubilantly at me. "He had a heart attack and now he has a fatal head trauma."

By the end of the class I am in my usual trembling sweat. The sheer physical exertion of becoming an EMT is something I never thought about. It seems we are always moving, stepping, squatting, pushing on someone. We have to be careful not to step on their arms or legs, to walk over their chest, to further damage the patient beyond what is already wrong with them.

The big rubber mannequins look so inhuman it is easy to forget they are supposed to be people. I find myself pulling them around by their faces, or reclining against their armless torsos during the breaks as if they were toss pillows.

It is always good to take a break. We are given one midway through the class. All the smokers run outside. I join them although I don't smoke. Frank smokes. He tells us that one of the big stresses for EMS personnel is bad health habits as he drags on his second cigarette.

I like it outside because the winter air is cold and dry and it wakes me up and dries off the sweat from working in the classroom. People still have not connected. There isn't the usual stoop chatter one hears among co-workers. People smoke in silence.

At the end of the class I get my coat from the hooks in the back of the room and leave. I am the last to leave because I have helped stack the chairs against the wall, something the cops demand we do. In the quiet parking lot I see someone standing alone by her car. It is Dot. She looks upset. I stop and talk to her. She tells me she thinks people in the class hate her. She seems so beaten down and miserable that I talk to her for what seems like an hour.

My hands and feet are freezing but Dot seems to be unaware of the cold. "No one wants to work with me," she moans. "When I join a group the guys completely ignore me or give me looks that could kill."

I don't know what to say to her, so I am honest. I'm not sure it is the best policy but I am too cold to think of anything better. "Maybe you should not raise your hand so much, just keep your opinions to yourself." Basically I am telling a bright person to act stupid. This is not going over well.

She starts to argue with me.

"Think of this like boot camp," I say. "The medics are here to weed out the weak. They want to break us down, so just get tough and don't take it personally."

As I am talking, one of the cops pulls out of the driveway in his patrol car. He yells, "Don't park in our spaces!"

Frank, who has packed up his lecture notes, pulls out in his SUV. "Good-bye, Frank," I call out and wave. He doesn't answer.

Dot still looks miserable. I ask her what EMS service she is joining after we graduate.

"Georgetown," she says.

The class is given its first test. I score an 80. I am devastated by how mediocre I am. I do nothing but study. This is a class filled with young cops and firemen, and I have a graduate degree from Yale. How can I be less than brilliant? I look at Dot's paper; she has gotten 100. Frank has even scrawled "good job" on the top. I am wild with jealousy.

Because Dot has claimed the seat next to me and she is left-handed, everything she has on her desk is aimed right at my line of sight or resting on my right leg. She is also a sprawler. I am anal about my textbooks, my pristine white notebook, the boundary lines of my desk and beloved windowsill where I park my coffee. She is always fifteen minutes late to class, rolls in unapologetically after Frank has begun the lecture, and throws her backpack down on the floor. She is in many ways my exact opposite. While I smile at everyone, she glowers. Dot looks rumpled, while now that my depression has been replaced by a feverish study of emergency medicine I have standing orders at the Georgetown dry cleaner for my shirts to be laundered with extra starch. Dot always wears jeans, a big ungainly windbreaker, and hiking boots. My cowboy boots are custom-made and my jeans well ironed. Her casualness is one reason why I am in despair that she has gotten 100 on the paper. "You got an 80?" she says.

She has stopped one micron before saying the words *I thought you were smart.* "It's not you," she says. "It is this test. It is a semantic mess."

As Frank lectures to us she scribbles wildly on her notebook so I can see it, something I haven't done since the seventh grade. Dot tells me she has a Ph.D. in semantics, and she goes into furious detail about every flaw in the questions. I appreciate her making an excuse for me. To her way of thinking, I am simply too smart to take a dumb test. I don't have the heart to tell her that the semantics really were not the problem, the problem was that I simply didn't know the answers to 20 percent of the questions. I imagine standing over a dead body in the back of the ambulance and telling the grieving family that it was not my medical error but merely a matter of semantics that I failed to save their loved one.

I am having a problem my shrink tells me is often experienced by first-year medical students. I have every symptom of every disease Frank mentions in the classroom. I am no longer clinically depressed but instead am dying of everything simultaneously.

Now I have fancy words for what is wrong with me. I am no longer sweaty. I am diaphoretic. My hand wanders constantly to my neck to check my carotid artery to see if my pulse is thready or bounding. I am no longer breathing rapidly but I am suffering from tachypnea. I have all the symptoms of a heart attack, a stroke, an aneurysm. I feel impending doom, my heart races, my hands tingle, I can't feel the right side of my face. When I am not enmeshed in my imminent death from medical problems, I am obsessing about all the impending scenarios of trauma waiting out in the world.

A car is not fun to drive anymore. It is a metal cage waiting to kill me in a dozen ways I have never thought about. I can get trapped inside underwater. The rescue personnel will not be able to free me thanks to Ralph Nader, a man I once admired but who now, as all EMTs know, is clearly Satan, having been responsible for cars whose doors do not fly open in a crash and come with safety glass that can't be shattered easily to free the victim. When Nader's name is mentioned the paramedics and firemen sneer and make the same spitting noise my Jewish grandmother made at the mention of the Nazis.

Terrible things can happen in cars. The seat belt can crush my intestines, my head can hit the dashboard and send my brain bouncing around inside my skull like a

Pac-Man figure under siege. It isn't just cars. After about ten classes everything in the world has become an accident waiting to happen. Dogs have teeth that cause severe puncture wounds, the propane gas tank on our outdoor grill can explode and level the whole block. Have a cocktail and you can get sloppy about chewing and choke to death on a hunk of steak. Bees can sting you and anaphylaxis can set in, causing you to suffocate. UPS trucks can carry up to seventy-five pounds of unnamed volatile chemicals. Babies and children are walking disasters, their big heads and delicate bodies designed for toppling, their large tongues for choking.

Frank stands before the class and tells us, "One out of twenty of you has a main artery that is congenitally faulty and will at some time hemorrhage. If you are lucky and it is caught in time, you will not die." He looks at me while he talks. I am now cyanotic, diaphoretic, and my pulse is bounding. "Stern, take your hand off your carotid artery," he says. "Pressure there can stop blood supply to the brain."

So what? I think. *I am almost dead anyway.*

By the twelfth class I see my notebook is filled with marginalia written from me to Dot and back. It bears the name of various physicians in the area. She wants to know who I use, who's good, who returns phone calls. Clearly she is dying like me.

The next class has me writing my shrink's name over and over in the notebook margin as a totem that everything will be okay. It says "TOM KNOX" down the page, as if those seven letters can stop fears the way Superman's cape does a speeding bullet. I have also written the word *bleech* in large wiggly letters—a word I haven't used since I was a kid and found the word while reading Don Martin cartoons in *Mad* magazine.

Bleech (pronounced *blek*) is a great all-purpose word of disgust. It comes in handy for class. We are learning about internal bleeding and feces, and how we have to see if someone's shit looks like coffee grounds, is dark and tarry, or gushing bright red. I think not.

I am at this point determined to specialize in shitless EMT events. I am also placing vomit on the no-can-do list. Frank tells us that a great many 911 calls will have us finding the patient in the bathroom, having taken a swan dive from the toilet. Sorry. But I will not do toilets. I begin to wonder if Georgetown will let me have a specialty involving only coming to calls where people are fully dressed and dry of ass. I am still thinking about blood as an option, but I have already decided that shit and vomit will not work for me.

Chad Howard has rescued us from Frank's odious world of "bleech." He is giving a class on the most innocuous practical subject: physical fitness. How not to strain our knees and backs while lifting people.

Chad is a young physical therapist. He is also a major hottie, blond and rippling with muscles and dressed in an endearingly dissolute preppy manner. Dot and I have pulled our desks closer together to better assess this situation. The margins of our notebooks are filled with lascivious scribbles. "He is WAY too cute," she writes to me. I feel like we are preteen fans of 'N Sync.

I ask her how old she is.

"40," she writes back. "You?"

I write "53." I am more than twice Chad's age. Dot and I don't listen to a word he says. We don't really need to pay attention to what he says; it is all written down in the instruction sheets we will get at the end of class. Instead we watch him squatting and lifting the Rescue Randy, and we see his corded tan forearms flex and the muscles in his thighs under his chinos expand as he shows us how to flex at the knees to save our backs. His cute butt is in the air, his shirt rides up to show six inches of smooth hairless back.

Frank is hanging out in the back of the room and looks like he desperately needs a smoke. He calls a break, and Dot and I swoon like schoolgirls, or maybe like vile old leering men at a topless bar.

When the class resumes Frank and Chad call on a volunteer to play an unconscious patient. My hand shoots in the air. Maybe I think Chad will lie on top of me and we can make out. I don't know what I am thinking, until I am lying on the linoleum floor with my eyes closed and I hear Frank tell the class that he and Chad will now hoist me in the air and place me in the stair chair (a piece of rescue apparatus used when a stretcher is too big to fit the surroundings).

I have for the first time in my life forgotten that I weigh a lot. I mean, I really weigh a lot. I never tell anyone my weight, I would never volunteer to have anyone gauge how heavy I am. The last time I even approached the situation of being airborne was twenty-five years ago when I weighed a lot less and a male friend and I were doing a jitterbug. He tried to lift me and swing me over his knee and after getting me six inches off the ground, he gave out with a huge grunt and collapsed on the floor.

Now for some unknown reason I have offered up my bulk to this young blond god, and Frank-who-I-think-hates-me. What is worse is that there are almost forty people as an audience to watch them try and hoist me in the air. I say the name of my shrink over and over under my breath like a Hail Mary.

It is easy for them to get me upright in a sitting position. I feel Frank's short muscle-bound arms wrap themselves under my bosom. He locks himself in, Chad grabs my legs. I am self-conscious about my legs, they are thick and heavy. All of me feels ungainly. I feel them give me a little tug to assess how hard they will have to lift. I feel my body's resistance as they pull me against gravity. I keep my eyes closed. I pretend I am dead or unconscious. The class thinks this is method acting but I am simply trying to disappear. Trying to will myself to be as light as helium. To my amazement I am suddenly airborne. It is a revelation. I honestly thought I was unliftable. I can feel them strain, but I am four feet in the air and then gently plopped into the stair chair. I peek out of one half-opened eye. No one is laughing.

I don't think I will become an EMT legend in the annals of the unbelievably fat. Already I have heard the stories about the 600-pound people who needed twelve firemen to lift them off the bed. I am ecstatic. I am again a seven-pound baby in her mother's arms. I am in love with Frank and Chad. I dream of them carrying me everywhere.

4

It seems that much of what we are lectured about in class is what *not* to do. "EMTs do not diagnose," we are told repeatedly. "Do not tell the patients they are okay, they may not be. . . . If a patient tells you he is about to die, do not argue with him; he probably will die."

I am already arguing this point in my head. When I feel sick, I get scared and I often think I am going to die. I was sure I was going to die on the stalled plane. If somebody told me I was probably right, I would likely now be dead from fright. How can I not diagnose, at least to myself? Someone has crushing chest pains radiating up their jaw and down their arm, they are sweaty, have a sense of impending doom, are nauseous, and have a pocketful of nitroglycerin pills. Is it a dislocated kneecap? Doubtful. If someone is telling me the Martians are talking to him through his tooth fillings, do I think he has appendicitis? Nope.

Chad the physical therapist comes back for the next

class. This time he is not lifting any of us but helping Frank lecture us about splinting broken bones. We are told that our firehouse will supply us with scissors for cutting people's pants off to see their injuries. Chad shows us a slide of a broken femur, the big leg bone in the thigh. In the picture it has not only broken but has pushed through the person's skin. It resembles the main mast of a sailing ship, stark and white, standing upright. The patient's pants flutter around it like a deflated sail.

Again I find myself noticing the ephemera of the scene. The man is wearing attractive gray flannel pants. I can't see his face or even upper body but imagine that he is a wealthy stockbroker who got in a car wreck driving his Lexus to the train station to commute into the city. Chad tells us that a broken femur can cause serious blood loss, enough to send the person into deathly shock. What we have to learn to do is to put the bone back in place.

The way we do this is with an apparatus called a Hare Traction Splint. The top end of it is wrapped with black Velcro bands around the top of the thigh, the foot is secured at the other end, and then with a crank like that of a medieval torture rack we pull the victim's leg apart until the broken leg bone is realigned. "You can expect the patient to complain," we are told. This I suspect is a serious understatement.

I am not taking notes; instead I draw pictures of a handbag I saw at Neiman Marcus, I draw crucifixes with jewels on them, I make a shopping list of food I need to buy for tomorrow's dinner. I am looking for comfort, for anything not to have to think about stretching a stockbroker's leg until his bones snap back into place.

Sometimes I think I am too stupid for this class. I cannot remember how many liters of oxygen is in an M-sized O_2 tank. Other times I think the class is too stupid for me. We are lectured on the following things:

1) Do not try to replace someone's organs if they are hanging from their body.
2) Do not give CPR to a severed head.
3) Do not try to revive someone who is in a state of advanced decomposition.
4) If you have a patient whose leg or arm is partially amputated, do not pull it off to make things "neat."

I wonder who would do these things: *I think the pancreas goes here; this looks like a gallbladder, let's shove it in here.*

I imagine myself doing chest compressions on a headless body from a car wreck and then running twenty feet down the highway blowing air into the mouth of a severed head. I scribble a note to Dot, who looks as aghast as I do. She seems to think that they are covering all the bases, I seem to think they wouldn't mention this if someone hadn't tried to do it.

I imagine myself as the Martha Stewart of EMTs,

pulling off ragged limbs to make the victim look more tidy. Maybe I could sew a calico edge along the wound, or crochet a lace trim on the cusp of an amputated leg, like I did with Soft Baby, my teddy bear.

Frank gives us one of the acronyms we will live by: DCAP-BTLS, which stands for deformities, contusions, abrasions, punctures, burns, tenderness, lacerations, and swelling. With the inevitable macabre slide show we see examples of each of the above. For abrasions we see a slide of someone who was wearing a T-shirt when he dumped his motorcycle at seventy miles an hour. Seasoned EMTs call motorcycles donorcycles because so many people die on them and their organs go to the waiting list of needy people. The man in the picture looks like Johnny Depp but he has no skin on his back. "Bad case of road rash," Frank says flatly.

In my notebook margin I have written a note to myself: "If you have to get up for air, just go." Underneath, I sign my shrink's name, imitating the unique loopy signature that I have seen on my prescriptions. And then another quote of his from his days as a medical student at Johns Hopkins. "You get used to it," he told me. I wonder if I will.

I look over at Dot, who is looking at the slide, her face a knot beneath her spiked hairdo. I look at one of the young firemen. "Gross," he says, followed by "Cool." He raises his hand. "Frank, do we get to see any autopsies?" That's it. I get up and run outside to the fresh air to die alone with dignity.

There are things I love in class and things I hate. I love bones, they are white and clean and make sense in their architectural order. I love mentally altered states; the tragic drunks and psychos appeal to me. I love splinting and taping and wrapping the patient in what is called "a hospital ready package." I like the cleanliness of white gauze and the four-by-four squares used to make occlusive dressings for sucking puncture wounds.

My hate list includes avulsions—big flaps of skin that hang like slices of corned beef from people's scalps. The birth of a baby in the back of the rig is supposed to be every EMT's happiest moment, but the movie we are shown in class of swollen pulsating vaginas disgorging placentas and pools of blood revolts me.

Dot, who has two daughters, digs childbirth. Because she and I will be on the same ambulance service, I write her a note and slip it to her: "I HATE this. . . . If anyone has a baby, YOU have to do everything."

"It's a deal," she writes back.

I am also ill at ease with the machinery involved in prehospital care. I have never been a technological person. When my computer fails or the TV remote malfunctions, I am clueless. I wander into Michael's adjoining office looking for help. Now I have to learn how to use machinery that will save people's lives. I can no longer afford to stand dumbly and stare at it like I do when the TV goes on the blink. I have to learn how to use a semiautomatic defibrillator, a machine that analyzes and shocks a person's heart rhythm back to normal. The machine, which is small and wildly expensive, is not nearly automated enough for my tastes. The *semi* in *semiautomated* means we still have to do things like turn it on and push buttons.

Shocking a person back to life involves shaving the hair off a patient's chest (hopefully men patients, not women or relatives of Bigfoot) to assure correct contact between the skin and the pads. We have to apply the pads in the correct places, check to make sure there is no pulse, press the button, and let the machine analyze the heartbeat. If it is shockable, we have to yell, "Clear," make sure no one, including us, is touching the patient, deliver the shock, recheck the pulse, do CPR, reanalyze, and reshock until the person is stable or still dead. It is a long process with great margin for error.

The goofiest thing is that the defibrillator talks to you, tells you what it is doing, and it has a built-in microphone that, when turned on, records every word you or anyone on the scene says. This is like having a spy in the ranks, someone who will rat you out if you make a mistake.

"What is the first thing you are going to say when you arrive at a scene and someone is in cardiac arrest?" Frank asks us. The class mumbles various answers. "*No!*" Frank says with authority. "You will all say, 'Oh, shit!'" We all laugh, and Frank tells us to think it, not say it, and not to verbalize anything like, "I have no idea what I am doing" or "I am too incompetent to do this job," because it will be preserved on tape for lawyers to have their way with for the rest of eternity.

Huge excitement. We are finally getting the stethoscopes and blood pressure cuffs that Frank has been promising us for weeks. They have arrived, and Frank, seeing the class's excitement, has started yelling at us in his loudest voice over the buzz in the room. "Listen up, people," he says, trying to shut us up as his assistant passes out the boxes that the medical supplies come in. Frank wants us to sit still like soldiers and open the boxes in unison, and let him explain the proper use of the things. But the class is wild with glee at the new official medical supplies. With a stethoscope around our necks we will look like real professionals, we will look like doctors on TV, like we stepped out of *ER*.

Dot and I decide we will take each other's blood pressure. I have never done this before, nor has she. "Me first," I say. She obligingly rolls up her sleeve. I notice how thin her wrists are, how small and white her arm is. Under her lumpy array of sweatshirts and down jackets she is tiny and womanly. I wrap the cuff of the sphygmomanometer around her upper arm, I place the stethoscope in my ears and the bell on the artery point near the crook of her elbow. I start to squeeze the bulb, I keep squeezing, I watch with glee as it rises, 110, 130, 160, 180, 200 . . . I keep squeezing. Dot is suddenly screaming in pain. Her face matches her maroon hair.

"Stop it, you're killing me!" she wails. I have no idea

how high to send the needle before I deflate it. I have no idea how to deflate it, I haven't found the metal screw that controls the pressure.

Frank is still trying to get control. "People, people, I need you to take your seats and listen to me," he is saying. Dot's wails are drowning out his words. I finally find the screw that deflates the cuff, she collapses chest-first on her desk and rips the Velcro cuff from her arm, which is now bright red. She accuses me of trying to kill her, to squeeze her to death like a python.

It is her turn. She squeezes the cuff in retribution, but I refuse to cry out in pain. "I can't hear anything," she says. "You have no pulse." I tell her she has the ear part of the stethoscope backward, and that she has the bell part turned around backward as well. She adjusts everything. Now she hears my racing pulse. "Your blood pressure is high," she says ominously. She tells me the number and I am surprised it isn't higher.

I can hear my own heart slapping against my chest wall. "Please God," I pray, "don't let any of my arteries explode until after the national boards."

The human head weighs between seventeen and twenty-two pounds. We are told this by Harry Downs, another paramedic, who shares the teaching load with Frank. Harry is very tall, talks in a commanding voice, and wears the uniform of a Norwalk Hospital paramedic. He has been doing this EMT job for a very long time, and amuses the class with stories from "the war zone." He has come to deliver the lecture that he immodestly says is "the single most important thing we will ever learn in the class." It is about the head and neck. He calls the brain's nervous system the Big Kahuna. He tells us that without it, the body wouldn't know to breathe, digest, regulate temperature, have a heart rate, or do anything else to sustain life. He gives us a dozen scenarios of hideous things we EMTs can do to screw up the head and neck. They all result in the same thing: irreversible paralysis, people who will end up unable to move from head to toe. One tiny movement of an injured person's neck the wrong way and you have made a quadriplegic.

The handwriting in my notebook has become neat again as an homage to the seriousness of this subject. "Spinal cords don't stretch," I write in my best penmanship, almost calligraphic. We learn about whiplash (hyperflexion) and what happens when you dive into a swimming pool and hit your head on the bottom, jamming your neck (hyperextension). We learn about hangman's injuries, the break in C1 and C2, the vertebrae that control the breathing nerves and the diaphragm's rise. We learn the danger of dangling from playground jungle gyms, from sledding, from football, from wrestling, from skiing. The big seventeen- to twenty-two-pound head that sits atop your neck is just waiting to be smashed like one of Gallagher's watermelons.

As if things could not be more dramatic we learn that men with spinal injuries develop a penile erection that will not deflate, a truly dire sign. I am obsessing about the permanent erection. Is this the silver lining to the dark cloud?

I am currently married to Xavier's head. Xavier is a young Mexican-American man who works as a night security guard and wants to be an EMT. He is very big, very sweet, and very shy. I never see him talking to anyone. He looks constantly terrified. The only time I have seen Xavier happy is when he had to lift someone in class. He is immensely strong, and it was effortless.

Harry Downs is showing us how to avoid making someone a quadriplegic. At the accident scene we are to hold the victim's head manually in a neutral position (that is, straight on) and then have another EMT apply a rigid cervical collar and transfer the person onto the long, rigid spine board. Once the patient is on the board, we secure the head with stiff foam blocks and straps or tape. The main thing is to never, ever, under any circumstances allow the head to move. One tiny shift might be all it takes to paralyze him.

"You are married to that person's head until you get them in a cervical collar," Harry barks.

My hands are buried in Xavier's thick black hair. I smell the lush tropical floral oil he uses on it. "Xavier, I am proud to be married to your head," I say to him. He blushes. I don't have the heart to apply the cervical collar as tightly as it should go. I am claustrophobic about such things myself and know this is only a test. I wrap it loosely around Xavier's bull-like neck. Harry comes over to inspect my handiwork. He sticks two fingers in the space between the collar and Xavier's tan flesh. He wiggles it, indicating that Xavier has room to move, room to become an instant quadriplegic. "You killed him," Harry shouts at me. "FAIL!"

5

By the midpoint in our EMT training we are laying hands on one another on a regular basis. We hear lectures and we take notes but we also spend a significant amount of time rolling, lifting, wrapping, splinting, and feeling each other's bodies, looking for imaginary bullet holes, leg breaks, and flash burns.

This Thursday is a special class. Instead of being at the police station we are meeting at the town fire department, where we will practice placing each other on stretchers or stair chairs and carrying each other down flights of stairs. Like second-graders going to a museum we are lectured by Frank to be on our best behavior. *"Do not touch anything. . . . Do not talk to the firemen. . . . Do not ask them questions."*

All thirty-two of us file silently into the firehouse at 7 P.M., our hands close by our sides. We resist touching the big shiny fire engines or gawking at the men and the equipment. We are led upstairs to the great room, where the stretchers and stair chairs are laid out with their straps. The firemen are even more annoyed than the cops by our presence. They sit in a semidarkened room watching HBO on their big-screen TV and mutter as we walk by. We are plebes, probies, maggots. We are invisible and meaningless beings.

There is no ladies' room, just a men's room with urinals and one stall. I have to pee. I walk in and find a fireman using the urinal; he glowers at me and I run out. We are not allowed to touch anything but no one said we couldn't look.

The decor of the upstairs of the firehouse is funny as hell. Miss Manners would have felt at home. New Canaan is a rich town with lots of old money and the firemen's private digs have mahogany piecrust tables, well-polished old silver loving cups, charmingly threadbare Oriental carpets, and tasteful wing chairs. It looks like the Yale Club with a few fire hats strewn around.

In this cozy collegiate atmosphere my worst nightmare is about to begin. My Achilles' heel in this class has been my age. I am over fifty and not in great shape. I know that much of this class is about brawn, about the ability to carry people down stairs, out of the woods, up from holes they have fallen into. One of our guest instructors is Anne, a woman paramedic from Norwalk Hospital. She is solid sinew from head to toe. When I wrap my arms around her midsection to practice the Heimlich maneuver I can feel her abdominal muscles beneath her uniform shirt. Even Frank, who looks to the casual observer to be out of shape, is as strong as a bull.

The first part of the class is not too bad. We load each other onto stretchers and four of us carry the "wounded" one around. By nine at night, after two hours of stretcher work, it is time to practice the stair chair. The stair chair is a folding chair used to carry someone in a sitting position down the stairs. It is useful for people who cannot be placed in a prone position or who need to be transported down narrow stairwells where a stretcher cannot go. Frank calls out our names. We are divided into groups of five. My group are all men, huge men. The biggest of them is Sven, a twenty-three-year-old Swede who is six feet six and weighs a good 250 pounds. Sven is teased in class about his formidable bulk. Frank decides I will be the one to carry Sven down three flights of stairs. To make matters worse, the lights in the stairwell have burned out or been turned off. I can't get a straight answer why the staircase is dark, but Frank insists that "it duplicates conditions we will encounter in real life." Sven will be placed in the stair chair and strapped in so his arms will not be free to reach out and grab the banister. I am to carry him down accompanied by one other member of the class.

With the stair chair you can be either at the head or the foot. To be at the foot means you have to walk backward down the stairs, in this case in a darkened stairwell. What Frank does not know about me is that I have no sense of balance. In my own home, with the lights on, in broad daylight, on a familiar staircase with broad carpeted stairs, I hold on to both the wall and banister when I descend. I have always had a phobic fear of falling. I am clumsy, I lurch about. Walking down stairs with no banister is impossible for me. Now I have to do it in the dark, holding up a giant Swede.

I opt to take the head so I can walk forward. I station myself behind Sven, who is strapped to the chair. Normally jolly, he now looks grim. He thinks I will drop him and he will tumble in the stair chair three flights down. "Don't worry," I lie. "I'm really strong."

Nobody, me included, wants to acknowledge that perhaps I should be trying to lift someone lighter. I refuse to whine. I bend my knees, place both hands on the hand grips of the chair. "On my count of three," I say to my partner, who has taken the foot end of the chair. "Three!" I yell, and with all my might lift this immense person high enough into the air to clear the steps. I walk down five steps. I start to wobble.

"Don't touch the railing," Frank yells at me. "Keep both hands on the chair or you will drop him."

I feel faint, I am falling, I can't breathe. "I have to stop," I yell, and Sven is put back down on the steps. I try to catch my breath.

Frank suggests that I take the foot part of the chair. I hate this even more, although he tells me it is a little lighter to carry the foot of the chair. It means I have to walk backward down the stairs. I am scared. Frank comes behind me and grabs the waist of my jeans to help guide me down. I am too polite to tell him he also has my undies and that he is giving me a major wedgie. He is going to steady me as I walk down the stairs; he will tell me when to step off.

"Lift" he says, and I bend over, my underpants tight in the crack of my ass. "Step," Frank says. I do not move. Sven feels even heavier holding him this way. *"Step!"* Frank yells at me. "Don't let him just hang in the air." Frank is pulling me down the darkened stairs by my underpants. Sven is swaying left and right. He knows he is going to be dropped. He frees a long arm out from the restraining straps and grabs the banister. I drop my end of the chair. Frank is still holding on to my pants. I hear a rip. Sven crashes down, groaning as he hits the concrete stairs. The four guys in my group all look away, embarrassed. "FAIL!" Frank yells. "Stern, see me after class."

I am bathed in sweat. My heart pounds, I can't breathe. I run past the guys on the stairs and look for a safe place to collapse. There is a couch in the darkened TV room where the firemen are congregated. I fall on the couch and they pretend not to notice me. I pull at my underpants; I try to breathe; I can't stop sweating. I start to cry. I think I am having a heart attack. What a way to go, surrounded by EMTs. I have crawled away into a dark corner like a dog to die. I can't call 911 because they are already here. I have failed, so why would they save me? Slowly I start to come around. I stagger to my feet and sneak out the side door and drive home. When I get there Michael is asleep. I don't wake him up. I stay up until 3 A.M. taking my pulse and blood pressure repeatedly. I press my carotid artery hard just as Frank warned me not to do.

That is it, it is all over. FAIL! The word rings in my ears. Move over and make room for the young and the strong, for women with six-pack abs, for giant Nordic gods like Sven. I can't even walk down a fucking flight of stairs without holding on. What good am I? What a waste of time this whole thing is.

The next day I call Melanie Barnard, a friend who is an EMT in New Canaan. She is small-framed and not all that young. I tell her my trauma with Sven. "Big deal," she says. "That's what the cops and firemen are for—to help you lift people." I am cheered: big, young, strong men, at my command. Suddenly I feel better.

At our next class I know I have to face Frank. Not only was I unable to carry Sven but I did not "see him after class" as I was told. Before class begins I summon up the courage to confront Frank with my FAIL. It doesn't seem to be as make or break as I thought it was. He looks at me somewhat sympathetically and says, "Do some weight training." It is not the end of the world. I buy a treadmill and do an hour a day on it while I watch *Trauma Center* on the Learning Channel to toughen me up to the gore factor.

Pretty soon my postclass routine of going home, having a bagel, and watching old movies on TV has changed. I am now watching the Tape. The Tape costs

$49.00 and is ordered through the mail from a medical book publishing company. The title is blunt: *Pass EMT-B*. We are now halfway through the class, we have about eighty hours of classroom work behind us and a dozen tests.

At the beginning of the last class Frank has brought up the subject of the national boards. We will have to pass this grueling two-day exam to become EMTs. The boards are given after all classroom work is done, after we have interned at a local hospital ER, and after we have passed Frank's finals. We then drive an hour and a half away to a vocational school in the boondocks of central Connecticut, where we are given the two-day exam. Frank tells us the odds of us passing it are 50/50. He tells us that many of the people we will see there will have already failed the test once or twice and are trying yet again. He tells us that the trick to passing is to memorize every word he has said and every word in our textbooks and then to get a copy of the *Pass EMT-B* tape and learn it by heart.

I order it on Amazon.com the minute I get home from class. I pay extra for overnight shipping although the test is still months away. Dot, who is extremely thrifty, immediately starts asking me who we can borrow a copy of the tape from. Deceitfully I do not tell her I have a copy. I want it all for myself. At least for now.

On my home treadmill, I put the tape in the video machine hooked up to the TV in front of the treadmill. *Pass EMT-B* is a six-part play, the star of which is a tidy young woman with a Dorothy Hamill haircut who progresses through all six practical scenarios of the national boards.

Needless to say, she does everything perfectly. She is to be our role model if we want to pass. I hate her. I hate her robotic delivery and the way she looks so humorless. I hate how her polyester uniform pants do not make her ass look fat. I hate that I have to act just like her in order to pass the test. I watch the tape twice a day every day. I watch her hook semiautomatic defibrillators up to real people pretending to be patients. Frank tells us that our patients will be National Guard recruits, and that we are not to talk to them before, during, or after the test. To do so is an automatic fail, Frank says.

When I am not watching the tape I am sitting in class. Tonight's class is about head injuries, and I am thinking about the fact that my father had a steel plate in his skull and how it made him go into uncontrollable rages. I don't know much about how he was injured so badly, except some hastily explained story about how he was playing near the trolley tracks in Harlem when he was eight years old.

As I child I never questioned the story or wanted to know more. My father was a very private man, and plagued by mental problems. When we sat together at Saturday-afternoon matinees at the Loews theater on East Eighty-sixth Street he clicked his tongue and hummed and cracked his knuckles and made weird ticlike facial movements. I could see the unevenness of his skull illuminated by the movie screen; his forehead caved in slightly and then came sharply out, where the plate must have been. For years I dreamed about Frankenstein's monster chasing me. I especially hated the big ragged stitches on his head. I always went to my mother for comfort after a bad dream, never my father.

My father could be charming but was unable to hold a job. His unpredictable rages would sever ties as soon as he blasted his boss wherever he was working. For a few years he stayed home, painted flowers and sailboats on canvas as a hobby, and waxed and rewaxed the family car. My mother supported the family selling handbags at a posh shop on Madison Avenue and then became a dental hygienist. When I was eight my mother packed some suitcases and ran away with me when my father was out walking our dog. We moved into a brownstone apartment thirty blocks uptown from where we had lived as a family. That summer my mother left me with our housekeeper and took a Greyhound bus to Juárez, Mexico, and got a divorce against my father's wishes. My father never forgave her, and as revenge he threatened to kill us both.

This is when my phobias started. I was afraid to leave the house—with good reason, I realize now. My father never actually attempted the murder, but he sat for hours at a time under the window of the brownstone where my mother and I lived. I could see him peering up at the window with binoculars. I kept waiting for the sound of heavy monsterlike footsteps on the stairs. Through the walls I could hear his hard breath.

*   *   *

I am finding myself growing more and more anxious as Frank lectures to us and shows us pictures of what a skull looks like after it has been whacked with a baseball bat and a steel pipe. Frank calls the brain the Big Cheese, his version of Harry's Big Kahuna nervous system. We are told not to be impressed by the massive bleeding that comes from skull lacerations, but to pay attention to assessing any visible bone fragments of the skull.

Frank teaches us how to use the Glasgow Coma Scale to gauge a person's level of awareness. He does not explain why it is called the Glasgow scale. I imagine unconscious Scottish people lying motionless on the cobblestone streets.

Frank is showing a picture of someone with dark circles under the eyes—the distinctive raccoon eyes of a neurological injury. The picture looks like me when I wake up in the morning after forgetting to take off my eye makeup. "The patient will present with the possibility of blurred vision, double vision, tunnel vision, ringing in ears, dizziness, loss of equilibrium, nausea, feeling that their hands are burning." I feel a menopausal hot flash starting, I am burning up. Dot is busy taking notes. I suddenly feel very cold and lonely.

I think about my father. He was born in New York City in 1899, when ambulances were still horse drawn. I imagine a crowd of people pulling him out from beneath the trolley and throwing him in the back of a wooden-framed coach. I wonder what hospital they went to and who the surgeon was. Was it a miracle that he lived? They didn't have EMTs back then, they had undertakers who would take you to the hospital. If you didn't survive the trip, your body went back with them to the funeral parlor.

I sneak a Valium out of my purse and swallow it dry. I make a note on the margin of my notebook to talk to Tom Knox about my father's head injury. I watch Dot take her left-handed notes. I reach out and touch the end of her jacket, which snaps me back to reality at the feel of it. Remembering that I am no longer a child is soothing, as is the reality that I have a husband like Michael to go home to. It is important to know that there will not be anyone waiting under the window to kill me.

6

May 13. That is the date of the national boards. I transfer this precious memo from the class bulletin board to my notebook, then write it on the back of another piece of paper and on the napkin for the caffé latte that I have brought to class. In case I lose anything I have backups.

As the class draws to its end the paramedics have become slightly more approachable. Frank's paramedic partner from the hospital stops by the class one evening. His name is Billy Mapes and he tells us a short history of how there were once no EMTs. In 1968 the Department of Transportation signed the "white paper," the original document that set out guidelines for what have since become the protocols and guidelines EMTs follow. It was also a way for the government to deal with the highly trained paramedics who were coming back from Vietnam with nothing to do with their skills. The 1970s were the birth of the modern EMT, the pioneer days, so to speak.

Frank and Billy stand in front of the class. They look like two thick bricks in the military-style uniforms issued to them by Norwalk Hospital. I envy the big gold-rimmed patches on their shirts. EMT-P, the highest rank. I like their snub-nosed military-style boots and their pants with extra pockets for scissors and notepads.

Billy goes to the back of the room, pours himself a cup of coffee, and sits as Frank finishes the lecture. "A—B—C," Frank drones. He is talking about radio dispatching, and even he knows it is boring.

"A—Accuracy: Know what you want to say before you say it.

"B—Brevity.

"C—Clarity: Don't scream into the goddamned radio!" he screams at us.

My head is filled with facts, facts I know and more facts I fear I don't know. They float like jellyfish in and out of my mind, nebulous and hard to grasp. Some moments I remember how the heart pumps, other times I see it as a big lacy valentine and am unable to recall a single thing about all the tubing that a real beating heart has hanging from it. I have become single-minded. I have no time to think about anything but passing the exams.

"If you pass my class, you will pass the national boards," Frank tells us. I pass his class, the written and the practical exams, and it is still a month until the national boards. I have become a walking factoid machine, spewing forth information about things few other people care about. When I am at Tom Knox's office I alternate between striking up bonhomie between two "medical professionals" and cringing at my lack of knowledge about the mysteries of the human body. I mispronounce words. I don't quite grasp concepts. I am not a doctor, I am not a nurse, I am not even an EMT yet. But with my stethoscope sticking out of my pocket, throwing around the terminology, I feel pretty cocky. I have gone from knowing nothing to knowing something.

Tom Knox shares medical school stories with me that I relish, about people passing out when they see their first cadaver, things like that, but I am afraid of the leap it is going to take to go from seeing gory slides in a classroom to seeing the real thing.

Michael cuts his hand on a shard of glass while lowering a storm window at home. I hear him cursing. I walk to where he is and make myself look at the injury. I feel faint. "It's different when people you know and love get hurt," Frank has told the class. I can only hope so, because the sight of Michael standing in the kitchen with blood pouring down his wrist is a hideous sight.

"I'll call 911," I say with some apprehension and some glee.

Michael rejects the idea. "It's not that bad," he says. The dish towel he is holding is now red. I tell him to apply pressure, which he does, and to elevate it. I get some ice cubes, put them in a plastic bag, and hold it outside the towel. The blood seeps awhile longer and then finally clots. We peel back the wrapping and look at the wound. It is long and deep, right above the knuckle.

"I really think you should go to the ER," I tell Michael. "I'll drive you."

He rejects the idea.

"I'm going riding," he says. "I have to see my horse."

He clumsily places a Band-Aid around the cut and heads out the door. I follow him. He gets in the car and I get in with him. We drive to the barn where we stable our horses, about forty minutes away from the house.

When we park at the barn I see the veterinarian's truck is there; he is inside giving shots and worm medicine to some of the horses. Michael brings his horse in from the paddock and starts to saddle him. His finger starts to weep red again. If I tell him three times to go to the hospital, it is officially nagging, so I say nothing. I am relieved to see Michael walk over to Ned, the vet, and remove the Band-Aid to show his finger.

"That's nasty-looking," Ned says. "Looks to me like you need stitches."

"Can you do it?" Michael asks. He trusts vets over most all doctors.

Ned shakes his head no and recommends Michael seek out a doctor soon.

Michael's horse, KT, is put in his stall and I drive Michael to a local storefront walk-in clinic. He will have no part of a hospital. From the waiting room I can hear him yelling in pain as the doctor puts in the stitches. I start to feel woozy again.

* * *

It dawns on me daily that very soon I am actually going to work with living people instead of mannequins like Rescue Randy. Before Frank's final exams, each of us in the class will spend a day at the emergency room of the local hospital. There we will assist nurses and doctors with anything they ask of us.

By the time my rotation comes up there have been ten or so people from the class who have been on hospital duty. The word back at the classroom is that life in the ER is dullsville. Hard to believe, but apparently nothing happens. One of the women from the class reported she filed her nails for hours during her shift, another read a book, another slept on an empty hospital cot.

I pick Monday as my shift day. I figure the weekend is when most activity happens and Monday will be quiet. I think it will be nice to have eight hours of downtime. I could use a manicure and some sleep myself. I bring my textbook with me to read and study for the final exam.

I am wearing a clean white shirt and pressed slacks. "No jeans," Frank has read us from the rules for the ER. When I get there the charge nurse is supposed to take care of us and tell us what we need to know. I present myself at 10 A.M. I can't find the charge nurse. The doctors will not make eye contact with me. I wander around peeking into the cubicles at the patients. Finally I locate someone in charge and announce my presence. They write a makeshift press-on label that reads JANE STERN,

EMT STUDENT, and stick it on my shirt. It does not inspire confidence. I try to look pert and helpful. I fall in step behind nurses. "Can I help?" I ask. They ignore me.

I am not helpful because I don't know how to do anything. They do not have the time or inclination to teach me. I feel like an interloper, and I am.

I try to look busy, I walk briskly from room to room. I greet the patients who lie in bed looking miserable. No one comes to a hospital ER on a Monday morning unless they are really sick. "Hello," I say brightly.

"I have to take a shit," someone moans at me. Another person is drunk and belches loudly when I come near him.

Another man, in the late stages of cancer, does not respond to my salutations. "I'll get your nurse" I tell them all, and walk away. The last thing I will do is tell the nurses what to do or where they need to go.

Monday is the busiest day in the ER. It is the time when everyone who has been sick all weekend finally gets in touch with their doctor, who tells them to go straight to the hospital, or when they finally stop biting the bullet and go because they are about to die.

My perky chatting with patients comes to an end soon. I am still in the way but the nurses are finding jobs for me. They do not acknowledge me, but just motion to me as an extra set of hands to help hold down a patient or administer a procedure—that's all I am given as directives.

"You," they call me. "Come here."

I have slung my stethoscope around my neck so I look like one of them. I am wearing heavy steel-toed boots that looked uniformlike when I put them on and now look vaguely Nazi-ish. I look like I am ready for guerrilla combat.

"You," the head nurse says. "Go to number ten and help out." Number ten is the curtain-draped cubicle in which a woman with advanced Alzheimer's and a host of other problems has been taken to the ER by her daughter.

"Hi, I'm Jane," I say to the daughter, who is my age. "What seems to be wrong with your mother?"

What seems to be wrong is that her mother, Alice, slipped into a coma a week ago. I look down at the bed. Alice has already been here for two hours and is hooked up to various monitors that beep and flash. Her eyes are closed, her white hair, in loose threads unraveling from a bun, falls around the pillow. She is old and small, childlike, actually.

"She won't wake up," the daughter tells me. She has been this way for some time.

I touch Alice's arm. I look at her chart. I see her name.

"Hello, Alice," I say.

Alice opens bright blue eyes and looks directly at me. "Hello," she says back.

The daughter lets out a scream, followed by cries to the Virgin Mary. "It's a miracle!" she cries. The nurse comes running into the cubicle.

"What's happening in here?" she says accusingly at me.

"It's a miracle," the daughter is still yelling. She points to me. "She brought my mother back."

The nurse glares at me. "What did you do?"

"Nothing," I stammer. "I just said hello."

The daughter has her arms around me. She is thanking the Blessed Virgin, she is thanking me. The commotion is causing a scene. I try to back out of the room.

"No, you can't leave," says the daughter. "You saved my mother."

I mumble something about being right back and take my miracle-working self away before more crowds of people form.

I am actually feeling pretty terrific. Maybe I am a healer of some sort, able to pull people out of comas. I stand in the center of the aisle as a patient on an ambulance cot is pushed into Room 6.

"You!" another nurse yells at me, breaking my moment of basking. "Come here." I float in, thinking another person needs my laying on of hands.

"Spread his butt cheeks," the nurse says to me, and pulls down the sheet. She is holding a rectal thermometer, and this is a three-handed job. I have never spread a stranger's ass before. The patient is having a seizure and an oral thermometer can't be used. I take a deep breath and grab a butt cheek in each hand and pull. She inserts the thermometer. We wait a few moments for it to register. I think of small talk to make. Nothing comes to mind. She whips out the thermometer and briskly walks out of the room. I am left holding the man's butt apart. I stand that way for a few moments and then realize it is probably safe for me to let go. I walk out to the sink, strip off my gloves, wash my hands, and reglove.

"Come in here," someone yells at me. In Room 4 there is a knot of nurses and orderlies. Before I go in I can smell booze. On the hospital bed is a man in his early forties. He wears an expensive suit, tasseled loafers, a gold signet ring on his finger, and a handsome, heavy watch. He was found passed out in his car on the Merritt Parkway heading into work during rush hour.

"We need to undress him," I am told, so I start helping the nurses get him out of his clothing and into a hospital johnny coat. This would normally not be too hard to accomplish except that this man is undergoing what the intern tells the charge nurse is "the worst case of DTs I have ever seen." The delirium tremens brought on from going cold turkey after a weekend orgy of booze and drugs have left our guy jerking around and levitating from the bed like Linda Blair in *The Exorcist*. "Call all the interns," I hear a doctor say. "They should see this."

"You," the nurse says to me. "Get him undressed."

I am left alone with this man who every five seconds thrashes his body into a position of rigor, then goes limp. An arm flails out, a leg. His head rolls from side to side. He is strapped to the bed, and like a magician I must denude him through his tie-downs. I manage to take off the suit jacket. It has a Paul Stuart label inside. The watch is a Breitling, his signet ring is from Harvard. I unbutton his shirt and between his thrashing manage to get it off him. He is now in a strap undershirt. I step back to catch my breath and take a good look at him. He is handsome, but I notice he is wearing fake bronzer that stops at his neck. His body is a funny yellowish color.

The nurse comes in. "What's taking so long?" she says. "Get his pants off, we have to take a rectal temperature." I yank at his pants, then his boxer shorts. "I'm sorry," I mutter to him because he obviously didn't start his day thinking he was going to be dying in the hospital ER with a stranger pulling down his pants. We turn him on his stomach and I spread his ass cheeks for the nurse. I now have a specialty in the wonderful world of emergency medicine.

The man is hooked up to an IV. A Chinese intern is injecting Valium in the line to try to stop his seizures. I like this intern because he is the only person so far who has conversed with me.

"Wow," he says when the drugs have no effect. "This guy is like an elephant, he needs so much sedation."

The doctor turns to get more drugs and I am asked to hold the man down so he will not hurt himself. I sit on his legs, because without my ballast the bed he is on rolls itself out into the hallway, that's how much he is rocking and kicking. He is slick with sweat; I feel like I am wrestling a large swordfish.

I watch the nurses go through his wallet. I look at the contents. A driver's license, a gold American Express card, some business cards, his business card. He appears to be an attorney at a New York law office. There is a faded dog-eared picture of him standing on a beach in what looks to be Hawaii or some other tropical paradise, with his arm around a nice-looking woman and two young boys in front of them.

"That's got to be his family," I hear the nurse say.

She disappears and comes back fifteen minutes later. I am still trying to hold him down so he does not injure himself.

"I got through to his wife: divorced. She doesn't want any part of him," she says flatly to an aide. "Says she has been through enough and that we should call his work if we need to talk to anybody. She seems to think he has no friends left who care about him."

The IV medicine has finally stopped his thrashing. He is relatively still. I speak his name, trying out my newly minted skill as miracle worker. He does not respond.

"Wheel him up to Intensive Care," says the nurse to an orderly.

"Do you think he will live?" I ask the Chinese intern.

"Doubtful," he says.

I watch the man being wheeled away to Intensive Care. I imagine the final call to his wife who doesn't care. To his boss. Will anyone come to his funeral? One of the strange things about emergency medicine, at least for EMTs, is we seldom know what happens to the patient after they leave our care. Our relationship with our patients is short and intense, there is no aftercare or follow-up by us. Sometimes the way we find out what happened is to read the obituary in the local paper.

The man with the DTs has taken an emotional and physical toll on me. I would like to sit down for a while but I can't. As soon as I spy a chair I am summoned by a nurse. "We need help in the isolation unit," she says. I am pointed in the direction of the holding tank for violent and mentally deranged patients, where a huge black man sits on the edge of a chair behind a glass screen.

The guard fills me in. "He is a professional karate teacher, he is schizo . . . tried to strangle his mother this morning."

"Oh," I say, at a loss for words. I watch him rock back and forth, talking to somebody in his head. The cops who brought him in have taken the handcuffs off and are now leaving.

"He needs to be taken up to the psych ward," the nurse tells me. I find a wheelchair and roll it up to the locked glass door. The guard opens his holding pen for me.

"Hi, I'm Jane," I say.

There is no response. He is too deeply engaged in talking to the voices in his head.

"I am going to take you for a ride upstairs to another department," I tell him as I roll the chair into the holding room. He stands up and sits down in my wheelchair. He is at least six feet four. He is wearing shorts and a tank top. His biceps are huge. I see he is drooling and working hard to keep up his side of the conversation with his inner demons. I roll him out of the locked room. I realize I have no idea where the psych ward is.

I roll the man through the ER. I ask the guard at the door where the psych ward is. "Four," he says.

I don't know where the elevators are. I find them. I don't know if I should use the elevators that are for the public. As they are the only elevators I see, I push the button and when the doors open, I roll him in. There are four other people in the elevator. Two hold bouquets of flowers; they are visiting sick people. One has a balloon that says IT'S A GIRL. My homicidal schizophrenic karate expert has taken this moment to play with his genitals. He rams a hand into his shorts and starts to masturbate. I smile at everyone in the elevator as if I am the perfume spritzer in a department store. "Four, please," I say to the man with the balloon.

All three people in the elevator jump out on two as soon as the doors open. I am now alone in the elevator with this crazy person. He has tired of his penis and now seems to be aware of my presence. I smile. I am terrified. "So you're into karate," I say. "That must be fun."

We get to four. I roll him out on the chair and push as fast as I can to the locked psych ward door. I knock. A nurse buzzes me in.

"Who is he?" she asks.

"He tried to kill his mother this morning," I answer. I have forgotten to take the pad with me with his name and stats on it. "He is psychotic," I pronounce.

The nurse gives me a withering look. "What is his name?" she asks.

"I don't know," I say.

"Well, go downstairs and get the paperwork, and why wasn't there a guard with you?" she asks.

"I don't know," I say.

She shakes her head. "It's your ass," she says as if to tell me that only a total idiot would get in an elevator with a crazed would-be murderer with no guards or restraints.

By the time I have gone back down to the ER, given the admission sheet to the psych nurse, and returned, all hell has broken out. A teenage boy and girl have been brought in by the paramedics. One of them is in very bad shape.

The trauma started out as the most routine of events. The pair were driving along a wooded road in a neighboring town. A deer jumped out, they braked hard, swerved, and their car came to a halt against a small stone wall. The impact forced the driver against the steering wheel. He was not wearing a seat belt. When the police arrived after a passing motorist called 911, the boy was standing by the side of the road, assessing the damage to the car. He was furious that his car was smashed in, but told the police that physically he felt fine. An ambulance had been dispatched and when it arrived the boy started to sign a refusal. He did not want to go to the hospital. In a few minutes he began to feel odd. It was hard for him to breathe. He thought he was having an attack of nerves. The paramedic put a stethoscope to his chest and listened. The boy was placed on a stretcher and hauled into the back of the rig along with his girlfriend, and with lights and sirens furiously blaring, they headed to the hospital.

The boy is suffering a bilateral hemopneumothorax, a fancy medical term that translates to the simple fact that his lungs have slowly collapsed after the impact of the accident and now he cannot breathe.

It is interesting to see how fast an ER is transformed into one big lifesaving machine when a life hangs in the balance. Suddenly the slow methodical triage of cases is turned upside-down with doctors and nurses shouting and calling out orders. The trauma surgeon is paged, and as we wait for him to arrive, the boy is placed on a bed in the trauma unit of the ER. The paramedics are working on him.

The boy looks like Axl Rose, lead singer of the rock band Guns N' Roses: a handsome, lithe teenager with long satiny hair flowing down his back.

He has been separated from his girlfriend, who is strapped to a spine board and wearing a cervical collar, awaiting treatment in another room. "Where's Sammy?" the boarded girl keeps asking. "Is he okay?"

Sammy is not okay. He is dying fast. His lungs have stopped functioning; he is trying to suck in air and it isn't working. Yet he is still able to scream in pain and thrash about wildly on the table. He is drowning in reverse. The nurses and paramedics rush in to hold him down, and the trauma surgeon appears. He takes his scalpel and holds it to the side of the boy's chest. The kid is trying to get up off the table. "Hold his legs down," someone yells at me. I look up and see Ralph, the paramedic who always brought the worst slides to our class.

I grab the kid's legs. The nurses have taken off his clothing. I noticed he has a smooth, lovely chest. It had been a while since I had seen a young man naked. He is beautiful and he is dying. How do you put those things together? I stand dumbly and hold his kicking feet. A few inches from my face the trauma surgeon slices the boy's side open and inserts a tube that will help inflate his lungs.

The head nurse is holding his head. She is talking to him as he screams for help, for the pain to stop, for breath. "You're going to be fine, honey, just hold on," she says. Her face is deeply furrowed with compassion. "You're going to be fine."

When his lungs start to work he stops kicking. "We don't need you now," I am told brusquely by the surgeon's assistant. I stagger back a few paces. I take in the scene, the knife, the blood, the tubes. I feel I should faint. I walk into the hallway to an area that will give me room if I do pass out. As I wait to faint, I don't. I am amazed. How can I watch what I just watched and still be standing? Maybe there is something in me that makes me able to do this. I go to the bathroom and throw water on my face. The crisis is over; the boy is being wheeled up to another part of the hospital. I can hear his girlfriend calling his name. I walk into the curtained cubicle.

"Where's Sammy?" she asks. She is clutching a CD

case filled with discs. "I have to go to the bathroom," she whimpers. "I'm scared."

I place my hand on her forehead. "Your friend is going to be fine," I say. "I'll get you a bedpan."

"I'm scared," she says again. "Are my parents coming?" I look at this girl. She has a tattoo of thorns around her upper bicep and wears a heavy-metal T-shirt. Her face looks like that of a frightened eight-year-old.

"I'll ask the nurse," I say as she holds on tight to her boyfriend's CDs.

By 8 P.M. my day in the ER is finally over. I go up to the head nurse but she is too busy to hear my good-bye. I wave at a few people in the beds waiting to see doctors. One nice lady has come in because she is burping a lot, another man is nervous that his heart is racing too fast. Like a candy striper in an old Gidget movie I fluff their pillows and make small talk, and then I leave.

I see Ralph Miro at the front door to the ER. "Hi," I say. He looks at me blankly. "I'm in Frank's EMT class," I say. Obviously he does not know me. "That was some hemopneumothorax," I say, trying again to bond with him.

"Oh, you heard about it?" he says. He obviously didn't see me, a foot away, holding the boy's feet down. "That was textbook," he says.

I float invisibly out the door and into my car. I am too edgy to go home. What will happen to all the people I met that day? What will happen to the coma lady, the lawyer, the karate guy, the teenager? I wonder if the nurses or doctors will notice I have left, signed out, shift over.

I already know the answer to that one. I am just a spare pair of hands that day. I have no name, no authority. I want to go home to a place where people aren't sick. I also want to turn the car around and go back to the ER. I am hooked.

7

I arrive at the national boards for my first day of testing with the joie de vivre of someone going to the electric chair. I am terrified. I have heard horror stories. Someone tells me that if you even turn your head to look at another student, you automatically fail. I am told not to bring a purse, not to bring my stethoscope or BP cuff, to bring photo ID to prove I am me, and to figure out a way to spend time between "practical stations" without talking to anyone or reading a book (no books allowed, as they may be cheat sheets).

It takes me two hours by car to get to the vocational school in Middletown where the test is held. I feel wildly out of place the minute I park the car. I see lines of young men, boys really, waiting to take the test. They have buzz cuts like the young public safety servants they aim to be. These soon-to-be-cops and firemen look trim and humorless. They also look worried as hell. I can't believe they have studied as hard as I have, but they all look like they could carry Sven down a flight of stairs without difficulty. To ease my mind I think that, unlike my psychiatrist Tom Knox and me, they do not look like doctors.

People say the practicals are the easy part of the test. Not for me. I am fine with a written exam, which you can take only after you have passed the practicals. I know about words, they don't throw me, but hands-on action with machinery is another thing. It is not my strong suit and today I will have six hurdles to overcome. Fail one and I cannot move on to the written exam.

It is now time to transform myself into the Dorothy Hamill girl in the EMT-B videotape, to regurgitate all my knowledge back to the instructor in perfect sequence. And so, for a whole day I go from classroom to classroom, where, with the aid of volunteers offering their bodies for me to splint, examine, bandage, and stop imaginary bleeding, I try to figure out why they were holding their stomachs, pretending not to be breathing, or pretending to turn blue.

I wear a white shirt and uniform pants to look "professional." It is a version of what I wore in the ER at the hospital. Unlike the girl in the video, my ass looks huge.

Weeks pass and I find out by mail that I have passed. Two weeks later, I am back in Middletown to take the written exam. This time I drive up to the same vocational school with Dot and Liz Jennings, another woman from the class. We plan to review all the way up. Dot has the study aid cards and reads the question, then gives the answer before we do. She keeps doing this. When she gets nervous she gets manic; when Liz gets nervous she becomes silent and tight-lipped.

Liz is a licensed helicopter instructor who wants eventually to pilot the Life Star helicopters that bring the seriously wounded to the hospital. The more Dot yells out the answers to the cards the more Liz shuts down, not talking as she hunches up in the backseat. I am trying to cram for the test and play social hostess at the same time. It is my car, and so I feel it is my job to make things pleasant. I tell Dot to stop giving us the answers to the questions right away before we have time to answer, but she keeps doing it.

We stop at Denny's for something to eat before the test. We have arrived an hour ahead of schedule. The booths are all taken so we sit at the counter, our nerves strung so tight that we can't figure out how to do this. We are like the Three Stooges: "You sit here. No, you sit here. No, you sit here." We keep getting up and exchanging stools with each other. The food comes and is borderline inedible. For some insane reason I order chili with beans, a bad choice before a three-hour test where if you go out of the room to use the bathroom you are not allowed back in. I take one bite; it tastes like dog food, so I eat the saltines that come with it and drink a Coke.

We pile back in the car and drive to the center. A group of our classmates have come early. They are the well-heeled contingent from New Canaan. They have actually prepared a tailgate picnic that they are serving from the back of the SUVs. They wave us over. We look like three nervous Third World immigrants. Dot with her purple spiked hairdo and wretched-looking parka, Liz wearing old blue jeans and a sweatshirt. I am wearing a long skirt, a cowboy shirt, and jangly earrings.

None of the tailgaters seems to be worried about the test. They are pouring Perriers and cutting Brie and pâté. They all wear pressed chinos and nice sweaters. They look like a Ralph Lauren ad.

I can't eat, I also can't be with Dot another minute, as she is driving me crazy. I go back to the car and open my textbook and spend the next half hour studying by myself. Why is it that nothing seems familiar at all?

The room in which the test is given is a huge auditorium. The proctor sits at a desk in the center and when the several hundred people have all been seated, he goes over the rules. Dot is trying to get my attention from two rows away. In my peripheral vision I see her waving at me. The proctor has just told us if we talk to one another we will be kicked out. I do not move my head an inch. She is calling my name and waving. I do not look. I can feel the Denny's chili moving around in my gut. I try to remember the names of the parts of the digestive system and draw a blank. The test is handed out. We take out our number 2 pencils and when the proctor says go, we open the test and start. In the huge auditorium we have been seated with empty seats between us, stripped of all purses, books, and study aids when we walked in. We are not even allowed to bring in a cup of coffee. My hands are shaking as I open the test book. We have three hours to complete it. I plan on taking the entire time, going over each question with lapidary precision. I take a deep breath and exhale.

I look at the first question. I have no idea what the answer is. I look at the second question: same thing. My toes curl in my shoes. I look down six more questions, and it is not until number seven that I know an answer. My stomach rumbles so loudly I can hear it. The only thing worse than failing the test would be to fail the test and shit in my pants. I hate Denny's, why did we eat there?

So I begin by answering the questions that I know, and when they are done, I go to the ones I think I know and answer those. By the third hour I have honed in on the ones I know I don't know. My memory has come back somewhat once the anxiety has decreased and I remember four of the first seven questions. The brain lock has lifted. By the end there are maybe ten questions to which I am still utterly clueless. I just mark the answer key in a pattern that looks pretty, hoping that graphically I have picked the right answers.

I go back over everything. Then again. I change one or two things. Two hours and 55 minutes into the test there are only six people left in the big room. The other five look really dumb. They are obviously "retreads," people who have failed the written test before and are back to give it another go. Finally, with a few seconds left on the clock, I get up and leave, handing my paper to one of the proctor's assistants. I rush to the exit and see Dot waving madly at me. "What took you so long?" she wants to know. I don't have time to answer. I rush to the ladies' room. When I reemerge the preppy contingent of the class asks us if we want to go out drinking. To my eternal gratitude Liz and Dot want to go home.

We get in the car. It is 9 P.M. and I am so exhausted I miss the highway entrance. Liz navigates while I drive. She talks in the all-capable voice of a professional pilot. I love her for this. I can hear her at the controls of a commercial jet that has just flipped over in the air. "Folks, looks like we hit a little turbulence," she would say. I tell her how much I hate flying, and ask her if she ever becomes a commercial jet pilot to promise that if I am on one of her flights she will land the plane and let me out if I have an anxiety attack.

When I finally get on the highway we start to go over the questions from the test. Liz thinks she has answered everything differently than we did. This means one of two things. Either Dot and I have failed and she passed, or the opposite. By the end of the two-hour ride home we hit a freak snow squall. I am crawling down the highway and I can't see two feet in front of the car. We realize that none of us remembers our answers correctly. We now have to wait six weeks until the National Registry of EMTs gives us (again through the mail) a thumbs-up or -down.

The next six weeks crawl by. I am on the phone almost daily to either Dot or Liz. "Did you get your mail yet?" we ask each other. I find a site on the Internet listing all registered EMTs. I check it every day for my name.

I wait longingly for the mailman. Like waiting for acceptance letters to college, you want to see that big envelope in your mail. The little one with only a letter in it is bad tidings. The big envelope has your EMT certification, your wallet cards, some patches that you sew onto your clothing, and a bunch of pamphlets from various professional organizations that you can now join.

Amazingly, Dot, Liz, and I all get our answers the same day. We have all passed. More than passed—we did exceptionally well. Our scores are broken down into categories, and while I have achieved a generally high score, to my chagrin I have gotten a perfect score, 100 percent, on obstetrics. Ugh. I don't tell Dot because should the occasion arise I still want her to deliver any and all babies in the back of the ambulance.

8

We are now EMTs, at least in the eyes of the state and of the nation.

But we are EMTs without a service to work for. So it is time to join the towns that paid for our training. Liz goes to Westport where she, like the New Canaan people, is given a fancy uniform and a shift with specific hours during which she must stay at the barracks waiting to be called out on the ambulance. Because she is new, she is put to work doing menial jobs like counting Q-Tips.

Dot and I present ourselves at the Georgetown firehouse on a Monday night. We are to meet Bernice Scherb, an officer on the ambulance and the person who will train us.

There is nothing Georgetownish about Bernice. She is tall, dark-haired, and chic, a former fashion model whose husband is a wildly successful corporate executive. She drives a new Lexus that has been customized so that at the flick of a button it morphs from being a luxury sedan into a sort of police car: the headlights strobe, blue lights flash on the dashboard, and her GPS tells her exactly where the emergency is. Bernice lives in a huge house in the fanciest part of town.

Bernice congratulates me and Dot on passing the exam and gives us each a pen she bought at Radio Shack to commemorate the occasion. It flashes the date and the hour in military time, something we will need to know for filling out the ambulance run sheets.

We are introduced to a few of the firemen and a few other EMTs who are hanging around. Dave Morris, a tall blond man who is both an EMT and fireman, gives us our pagers and shows us how they work. We are to keep them on our person all day and return them to their electrical housing at night, where they will recharge. These pagers will sound our tone and tell us what and where the emergency is if we are needed.

We are given numbers. I am G-65. Bernice is G-56. I just have to think of myself as Bernice backward: she is tall and slim, I am broad and average in height; she drives a Lexus, I drive a Subaru; she knows what to do in a real emergency, I know what to do on paper, but have not seen anything real yet outside the emergency room. Not a drop of blood, not a car wreck, not a gunshot wound.

I am beginning to realize that while the class was about taking a test and acting like the Dorothy Hamill girl, here at the firehouse it's about getting your hands on a really sick person and trying to save that person's life. Suddenly all my fears come back and I think I am way too claustrophobic to ride in the ambulance, to see anything icky, to get up at 3 A.M. from my warm bed. What am I doing here?

Now equipped with a pager, I am on call—two long tones followed by five short beeps means *get up and go*. It is exciting because I love nifty new gadgets and things like patches and badges, and being an EMT is a bonanza of stuff. Here is a short list of the stuff that I have acquired since I passed the test. Some of it was given to me by Georgetown, the rest bought with my own money from catalogs and police supply stores:

1) A two-way radio with a long antenna for my car

2) Flashing blue lights installed on the rear windshield ledge and on the front dashboard

3) Stickers that say EMT stuck on every side of my vehicle

4) Patches that say EMT sewn onto my clothing

5) An EMT jacket that says GEORGETOWN on the back

6) A jumpsuit that says EMT in reflective letters on the back

7) Two big flashlights

8) A "jump kit"—a medical supply kit that goes with me in my car to a scene, should I get there before the ambulance

9) A portable oxygen tank

10) A fireman's jacket and pants and a real fire helmet of the old school with a big leather patch on the front

11) A modern EMT helmet, sort of like a motorcycle helmet to wear on scene in automobile crashes

12) A box of nonlatex gloves

13) A handful of protective breathing masks to wear over my nose and mouth

14) Plastic eye goggles to keep blood and debris out of my eyes

15) A fabulous switchblade knife with a serrated blade

16) Scissors to cut clothing off people

17) A bright orange reflective vest to wear for directing traffic

18) A huge star of life emblem that signifies EMT and covers nearly the whole hood of my car

19) A front license plate for the car that says GEORGETOWN FIREHOUSE and EMERGENCY MEDICAL TECHNICIAN

20) A new, more expensive blood pressure cuff and stethoscope than the ones we were given in class

21) A silver badge for my wallet that identifies me as a member of the Georgetown Fire Department

There is a line between enough stuff and too much stuff. The big star of life sticker that goes on the hood of my car was my idea, not issued to me by the firehouse.

With it I have crossed that line and gone over the edge, from a humble probationary member into the dreaded category known as a "spanker" (as in spanking new): an EMT who flaunts his position by having too much stuff.

Of course, if anyone had asked me, I could have given a good reason for applying the two-foot sticker to the hood of my car. Unlike the good old boys and Bernice, who are known to all the cops in town, I want everyone to know that I belong there when I arrive at an accident scene. My sticker (which I purchased from Galls, a phonebook-thick catalog of stuff for cops and EMTs) looked discreet on the printed page, but when it arrives even I am aghast to see that it is in fact larger than the one on the ambulance—though not so aghast that it stops me from applying it to the hood of my car.

The sticker becomes a firehouse joke: not just at my firehouse, but at the two other firehouses in the neighboring towns. I am the New Girl with the BIG Sticker. And, to my chagrin, the huge sticker is visible to every person in the world but the cops, who still refuse to recognize my legitimate presence at an accident.

"Nice sticker on your car," guffaws Bob Withall, a Wilton town cop. "It looks like the landing pad for the Life Star helicopter."

I am in love with my sticker and leave it on despite the razzing. Like the owner of an American Express Platinum Card, I am convinced that it commands "worldwide respect."

I walk around the town and go grocery-shopping in

my fireman's coat. It is as spanking new as its owner. I wear it to a meeting of a women's group that I belong to. I hear hushed whispering. I think people are in awe of my new affiliation, the fact that I am now officially a member of a fire department. I swell with pride. When I get home there is a message on my phone machine from a good friend. "Jane, if we didn't like you so much we wouldn't say anything, but we are afraid that someone sold you a fireman's jacket as a winter coat."

Sooner or later it had to happen, and it happens sooner: my tone goes off and I am on my way to a real accident. Two things go wrong straightaway. First I get on the two-way police radio and give Bernice's call number instead of mine. She has already signed on the call, and so the dispatcher is surprised when someone else identifying herself as G-56 signs on a minute later. My mistake dawns on me and I correct myself. "I mean G-65," I say, and then commit the worst possible breach of police radio etiquette, which is to start apologizing and chattering away.

To say one word more than necessary on air is to be at the very bottom rung of spankerhood, a fool. One is supposed to act like Joe Friday of *Dragnet* on the radio, not some yenta on her home telephone.

After I have screwed up my first radio transmission, I realize I am out of the driveway, blue lights flashing, driving eighty miles an hour, and I have no idea where I am going. I have lived in this town for more then twenty years and have not once noticed the name of any street other than the one I live on. Like most people who live in a fairly rural place, I know the roads but not any of their names, and I know who lives where but not their formal addresses. Now I have to find the road by its official name, the house by its "numeric," then figure out how to park near enough to the house to drag all my stuff inside but not so near that I block the space where the ambulance will pull in.

I am a symphony of missteps. I am trying to put on my rubber gloves as I drive, look at the map issued to me by the department, and drive faster. I am a worse accident waiting to happen than the one I'm going to. It is ten at night with no moon. I can't read the map because I have forgotten my reading glasses, I am swerving all over the road, I keep clicking the transmission button on the radio, to the palpable irritation of the dispatcher, and asking for directions—another cardinal sin. One is expected to know the roads of the town by heart.

I find the house. I throw on my EMT jacket, grab my jump kit, and run to the front door. Bernice and the rest of the crew have gone to the firehouse to pick up the ambulance. I am the first one on the scene.

The call is for a seventy-four-year-old lady who has fallen. I arrive at the front door on this chilly winter night in a sweat. I must look frantic. Personally I wouldn't allow me in the door. The lady's son ushers me in. "My mother tripped," he says. "She caught her foot on the bed frame and fell. I think she has broken her hip." I am shown the way upstairs to the tidy bedroom. A large crucifix hangs over the bed. In the room there is a knitting project under way, what looks like an Irish fisherman's sweater. The room is clean and sparse, with a few framed photos of young children and an old-fashioned vanity set with a silver-backed brush and mirror on a table. The patient is lying next to the bed. She is pale and damp and obviously in extreme pain.

"Hello," I stammer, "I am Jane with the Georgetown ambulance."

I have already forgotten her name, although her son gave it to me at the door. I can't remember if I am supposed to examine her first or fill out the information pad. I call her "Mrs.," like a cleaning lady might do. "Mrs., tell me what happened," I say. I already know what happened. Her son told me, she tripped on the bed leg and fell. I am wasting time because I am scared to touch her. She is able to speak and tells me what I already know.

"On a scale of one to ten," I ask, "how bad is the pain?" We were taught to do this, so I am on the right track.

"Ten," she answers.

I know that's a bad sign, but now what do I do?

She is fully dressed. I attempt to see what she has done to herself. "I'm going to take a quick look," I say, as if I have been doing this all my life. I try to find a place on the carpet that is not covered by the medical junk I have brought in and strewn about.

I do what I was taught not to do: I step over the patient. I step in such a way that my foot kicks her hip. She screams in pain. I am paralyzed with fear that I have now made her injury worse. Perhaps she will sue me, or maybe she will die because I did this. I am sweating like a pig. I throw my jacket to the floor.

"Let me take a look at your hip," I say. I remember I am supposed to check for deformations, contusions, bones out of alignment. I give the gentlest tug on her polyester pants. "Mrs.," I say, "I will try to be as gentle as I can be." (Why would she believe me, as I have already kicked her?)

"My mother has osteoporosis," the son says. This old lady is brittle end to end. "She has already broken her leg and her arm this year."

I ease her pants down below her hips. She is wearing a full girdle, and something puffy pouches out at the bottom of it.

"My mother is incontinent," the son says. I now see she is wearing an adult diaper.

I would have to cut the girdle off to see her hip. So I leave that alone, afraid to make things worse.

"Mrs., I am going to take your blood pressure," I say. I reach into my jump kit and pull out the cuff and stethoscope. I try and gently pull her sleeve up.

"My mother has had a double mastectomy, both sides," the son tells me.

"Oh, I'm sorry," I say, remembering that you do not take a blood pressure reading on the side that has had the surgery. What about surgery on both sides?

I lean over her, jostling the bad hip again. I decide that I will have to take a reading somehow so I wrap the cuff around one of her arms and pump to inflate the thing. I look at the gauge and realize I do not have my glasses on and cannot see the numbers. I squint, trying to get a reading. I reach down to take her pulse and I am not wearing a watch. I hold her hand: she squeezes my hand hard. She is in a lot of pain but she is a trouper. I admire and like this lady; I want to apologize to her for having gotten me as an EMT.

I attempt to take a pulse. I find the beating heart echoed in her brittle wrist. I hear the beat but without my watch it is useless. "Never make anything up," I hear the voice of Frank from the classroom in my head. I want to make up a pulse and a BP number as I hear the siren of the ambulance pulling into the driveway. I am grateful for their arrival and also aghast at what they will think of me. I have been on scene for ten minutes and have done nothing for this woman except kick her in her hip.

Bernice comes into the room. She has her game face on. She is calm and cool and asks in a soothing tone, "What's the matter?" She starts doing a trauma workup on the patient smoothly as she crouches next to her.

"Did you get a pulse and BP?" she asks me in the same calm voice. Clearly I am wearing my stethoscope and have the blood pressure cuff in my hand.

"No," I say. Frank would be proud of me: at least I am not a liar. Bernice seems confused. I know she must be wondering what I have been doing with this patient.

The firemen and other EMTs load the woman on a long board, secure her to it, place her on the cot, cover her with blankets, and take her out to the waiting ambulance.

"Jane, do you want to ride with us?" Bernice asks me.

I am hit with the reality that sooner or later I will be expected to actually get in the ambulance with the patient. This is so difficult for me that I have spent a few sessions with Tom Knox trying to figure out if I can simply drive behind the ambulance on the way to the hospital rather than actually getting inside of it. Neither of us can figure out a practical way for me to do this, so instead we have switched gears and talked about what it will be like when I finally step on board. I don't want it to be like the plane I was stuck on, or the bus I was afraid to ride. I am hoping that I can step outside my own head long enough to think about the patient and not about me. But I am not there yet.

My mouth is dry from fear. I shake my head no. "Not now," I say to Bernice. "I have company at my house." Frank never said that we couldn't tell social fibs.

I just want to go home. I am afraid of climbing into the back of the ambulance. I am afraid my claustrophobia will surface and in addition to my being professionally useless they will have a second patient on their hands, a nutcase who wants to pull over and get out.

The ambulance pulls out of the driveway.

The night is dark and quiet. With the noisy ambulance gone, it is just me and the lady's son, who is locking up the house as he prepares to go to the hospital.

"I hope she will be fine," I say, wrapping the blood pressure cuff up and tucking it into my capacious jacket pocket.

"Yes," he says gravely. "I want to thank you for all your help."

I feel like a thief who has been caught red-handed. I just nod.

"Thanks," he says again.

"Thanks for nothing," I mutter under my breath as I walk to the car. "You're lucky I didn't kill her."

It is a day later. I have just drifted off to sleep when the tone goes off. It jars me from the deep sleep that we all fall into when we first lose ourselves in dreams. Two long flat tones, five beeps, then the voice of the dispatcher calling, "Georgetown Ambulance personnel, car versus motorcycle on the corner of Route 107 and Route 57." I look at the clock. It is 11 P.M. This location is about half a mile from my house, near a local bar. I jump up, suddenly struck by two pressing urges: the urge to pee and the need to get dressed and out the door fast. I choose the latter. I grab my jumpsuit and climb into it, then stick my feet in the first available pair of shoes. I am wildly patting myself down to see if I have my watch, my eyeglasses. I flick on the pulsing blue lights in the car and then the radio. Miraculously I give my correct number, G-65, instead of Bernice's. My mouth is again parched and dry. I hardly have enough saliva to speak. I drop the microphone on the floor, pick it up, and say my number again. "Roger, 65, heard you the first time," says the dispatcher.

Fortunately, the ambulance has beaten me to the call and as I pull in and park on the side of the road, I survey the scene. The local cops are diverting traffic around a slightly dinged car and an extremely creased motorcycle. The motorcycle driver and a woman passenger are sitting up on the pavement. They are not wearing helmets, and as I walk closer I can tell they are both shit-faced drunk. The cops are talking to the driver of the car, who is irate at the motorcycle driver. "He just peeled out in front of me, I couldn't stop."

The bike is a massive new Harley, now reduced to junk. The windshield has left little shards of glass all over the road, the bike has dumped the passengers and then hit the guardrail. It is twisted and useless. I walk closer to the driver of the bike. He is trying to stand; the firemen are holding him down so Bernice can put a cervical collar on him in case he has broken his neck and is too drunk to notice. He is moaning, not from pain or for his girlfriend, but for the Harley. He wails in a high-pitched yelp like an angry coyote. I hope he starts to rend his garments, as it will save me from having to cut them off. I can smell him and his girlfriend from ten feet away.

Bernice is joined by Mike Cappello, a senior EMT, a silver-haired, slim, unflappable guy.

"They're drunk," I offer my professional assessment.

"I know," Mike says. "Jane, go to the rig and get the frac pack."

I run toward the ambulance. I come to a halt. I have no idea what a frac pack is and I don't know where it is. I trot back to Mike.

"Where is the frac pack stored?" I ask. I don't have the nerve to ask him what it is. If he tells me the location then maybe I can fake it.

I rummage around in the compartment he has directed me to. I see all sorts of things. "Frac pack," I mutter, hoping it will answer me. *"Right here!"* it will say.

My mind starts to cogitate. "Frac . . . fracture," I think. This is like a game. Fracture pack! Okay, Mike wants the duffel bag filled with all the splints and cravats to package the drunk biker's broken limbs. I pull out the duffel bag and run back to Mike.

"Here." I hand it to him as proudly as a hunting dog with a downed bird in my mouth.

He throws it back at me. I am not his gofer, I am an EMT. He wants me to splint the guy. I rummage around in the bag and come up with two leg splints. The biker's right leg is twisted badly, obviously broken. "Cut off his shoe," Mike directs me. I take out my blunt scissors, but they're no match for a motorcycle boot. I saw at it, cut the laces and straps, and finally it comes off. I brush away shards of shattered glass, I pick gravel off his pants. I take a pulse in his foot to see if he has circulation. I notice out of my peripheral vision that Bernice and the cops are working on the woman passenger. She is now sitting up, smiling, happy as if she just won the Publishers Clearinghouse Sweepstakes.

The paramedic appears. He jumps in to survey the scene. He looks at the smashed bike and then at the bikers. They are in amazingly good shape, considering. I think of the old adage that God protects fools and drunks.

We are going to transport both of them to the hospital. The guy, who is the more bruised and bloodied, goes on the cot, and the woman on a long spine board that is placed on the cushioned seat on the side of the ambulance. Two passengers, a paramedic who will ride with them, Bernice and . . . who? . . . me?

"You go," Mike says to me. I think he knows I am about to come up with another excuse why I can't get in the ambulance.

The two motorcyclists, Bernice, and the paramedic are in and waiting for me. I make a tentative step toward the rig.

"Let's go," a voice from the driver's seat yells. I pick up the pace. I grab a side rail and hoist myself into the vehicle. I feel like I am pulling a great weight against gravity. Someone slams the big metal door behind me and I feel the rig jump-start, lights and sirens flashing. We are moving.

I am ambivalent, to say the least. I am proud that I am inside, but I don't want to be there. It's like being trapped in a crowded elevator with a bunch of strangers. In this case two of the strangers are bloody and drunk.

It is night and the neon overhead lights cast a greenish stark glow on the inside of the rig. Suddenly I know I'd better find a place to position myself because I am about to fall over. The ambulance is going at a moderate clip, but from the backseat it feels like a roller coaster. We are hitting potholes and curves I never knew existed on this road before.

I am not part of the team. I am an outsider looking at what is happening. I stand mutely hanging on to a metal bar on the ceiling, trying not to fall. It is like getting your sea legs on a ship in the middle of a storm.

"Cut his jacket off," the medic says to me.

"Okay," I reply. "By the way, my name is Jane," I say politely. Silence. He doesn't care what my name is, he has a job to do.

I pick up a pair of scissors and start to hack away at the thick black leather jacket that the man is wearing. We can't take it off him in the regular manner because he must stay immobilized on the spine board.

He is drunk, but not so drunk that he doesn't know I am about to ruin his beloved biker jacket. "Get away from me, you bitch," he yells. "Don't touch my leathers."

"Get the jacket off," says the paramedic. I start to cut again. The man screams at me to leave him alone. I decide I'd better listen to the paramedic, who needs a bare arm and access to a vein to start an IV line.

"My leathers, my leathers," the biker moans as I reveal his arm bit by bit.

"Don't do that," I hear a voice from the padded side

bench wail. It is his woman friend, whom Bernice is examining for trauma wounds. I assume the girlfriend is hurt and Bernice has touched something painful. But I am wrong. "Don't cut his leathers," she moans at me.

I pay no attention to her, I do what I can do, which is to cut with a blunt scissors. It is slow going. I have a sharp knife in my pocket that I know would slice the jacket off in a second, but I can hardly hold myself up from falling in the back of the rig, and all I need at this point is a big unsheathed blade to do damage with. I imagine myself falling on the patient and stabbing him to death.

Despite the commotion, I get the arm exposed. The medic taps a vein and plunges a needle into it. He hooks a bag of saline to a hook on the ceiling and starts an IV drip. In this chaotic madhouse I realize a few things. Within a few minutes the two people are neatly hooked up to IVs, they are both wearing oxygen masks, they have been gone over thoroughly, and their bruises and bloody parts have been assessed and attended to. There is a sudden calm in the rig. They are two very lucky people, neither one seriously hurt, just surface cuts and the guy's splinted leg.

"Jane, start filling out the pad," Bernice says as she passes me the small white pad that contains all the very basic information we will need on a patient: name, address, date of birth, allergies, medications, blood pressure, and pulse.

I ask the biker his name. The booze he has drunk has

made him mumble, and the oxygen mask further muffles his speech. His woman friend is receiving oxygen through a nasal cannula, so she can talk more clearly.

"What's his name?" I ask her.

"Bozo," she giggles.

I start to write on the pad and stop, realizing this is not a name. "What's his real name?" I say.

She finds the whole situation a riot. She is convulsed with laughter. When she stops laughing, I try again. "His name, please," I ask.

"I don't know." She shrugs.

"Is he your boyfriend?" I ask her. I think maybe she is his daughter, he is at least twenty years older than she is.

"Yeah, we've been dating for five months. But I don't know his name. I just call him Bozo."

I am dumbfounded. "Look in his wallet," says Bernice. I pull the wallet from what remains of his jacket. He has a name. He also has a gold American Express card, and a business card that identifies him as the president of a small local business. He is a weekend motorcycle warrior, and his girlfriend must come with the "Saturday night at the bar" outlaw package.

Finally I am doing something I can do. I am writing words on a pad of paper. I have done this before. I neatly print his name, his address, and take the vitals that Bernice has just taken and write them on the pad.

"Are you allergic to anything?" I ask.

"Mmpph," he says through the oxygen mask.

"Do you take any medication?"

"Ggrrtt," he slurs.

I think to ask his girlfriend, but the odds are that if she doesn't know his name she won't know his medical history. I leave the spaces blank.

"Change seats with me," the medic says. We do a precarious ballet in the back of the swaying rig. We climb around the patient so the medic can sit next to the two-way radio with which we call the hospital. We are five minutes away from the ER and he is going to make the call to tell them who we are bringing in and the extent of the injuries.

I sit in the new seat and take a deep breath. All is calm. The patients are stable and packaged, ready to be rolled out for the ER staff. I have made it. My maiden voyage in the back of the ambulance. I was so busy with things to do, I didn't have time to worry about my sanity.

I listen to the medic call in. He gives our location, tells the ER the patients' vital signs and the level of trauma so they can prepare as needed. The biker looks sleepy and calm. I pat his leg that I have bandaged, adjusting the tape a little so it looks textbook perfect.

Something is wrong. I am sitting in a puddle of liquid. The first thing that I think is that I have peed in my pants from nervousness and am now just starting to notice. But the pee is cold and increasing quickly, and I know I am not actively peeing.

With the medic on the radio and Bernice busy with the girlfriend, I sneak a look. I rise up a few inches and look at where I am sitting. I see the problem. When I changed seats with the medic I pulled the IV line out of the man's arm and I am now sitting in a puddle of saline. The needle is still stuck in the man's arm, but it is delivering nothing. The liquid is flooding around my ass.

I grab the tubing. "Hey, this just happened," I lie. "It must have pulled out when we went over that bump." The medic quickly adjusts the tube, reattaching it to the needle. He doesn't scream at me, for which I am eternally grateful. I wonder what people will think when I stand up and they see that the seat of my pants is soaking wet.

"Okay," Bernice says as we reach the hospital. "We're here."

The ambulance driver backs in, and the rig makes beeping noises like a truck does. It comes to a stop. There is a flurry of action. The big doors are opened from the outside. The biker who is on the stretcher is taken out first, a second stretcher is brought around, and the girlfriend is transferred onto it. The cots are head to head. She reaches out and touches him.

"I love you," she purrs. "I can't believe they cut your leathers."

"Mmmmmph," he says back.

We wheel them in, find the cubicles assigned to them, and hand them over to the nurse. We give her the basic information, and then take the long and intricate run form to the little desk that the EMTs share to fill it out. I watch Bernice fill it out at lightning speed. As she is doing that, the driver is disinfecting the rig and making up the cot with clean sheets.

"Is there a ladies' room?" I ask Bernice. She points me around the corner. I semistagger over to it. I just need to be alone by myself to process what just happened. I catch sight of myself in the mirror. I am an amazing mess. Without even taking my wet ass into consideration (the over-the-sink mirror doesn't reach that low), my face is bright red and I am sweaty and disheveled. I pull off my surgical gloves and sweat runs down from the inside. Splashing water on my face helps a little; at least I am now wet all over.

By the time I emerge from the ladies' room, Bernice has filled out all the forms and has even made her trademark courtesy call to the patients before we leave. It is a nice touch; she always goes into their cubicles and says good-bye, to make sure they are okay.

I flop along beside her, shaking and wet.

We head back to the waiting ambulance, parked outside the ER. I climb into the back with Bernice. The paramedic's car has been driven to the hospital by one of the firemen. In the back of the rig the lights are now lowered; it resembles a medical cocktail lounge, dim and antiseptic. Without the distraction of a patient my mind starts to think of claustrophobia and other reasons why I shouldn't be here.

"Dunkin' Donuts or McDonald's, ladies?" comes the voice from behind the steering wheel.

"Doughnuts," Bernice and I call out in unison.

How scary can this be if we get to eat doughnuts afterward? I think of what I am going to eat. My ass is drying. I like the neatly folded blanket on the cot, and the smell of the disinfectant.

"Good job," Bernice says to me.

I feel flushed with happiness.

"I did it," I tell Tom Knox during my shrink session. He smiles broadly as I tell him how I was able to sit in the back of the ambulance and not freak out. "I knew you could do it," he says. I inhale the comforting aroma of his office, I try to fix it in my mind to pull out like a snapshot for when things get rough.

9

I have been so focused on the ambulance that I have forgotten that I am now a member of a fire department and I have about thirty-five new people in my life that I have to get to know.

Life at the Georgetown firehouse runs by a schedule. Every Monday night there is a meeting. The first Monday of the month is a business meeting where the secretary reads the minutes of the last meeting and new business is attended to. On the other Mondays we have drills, which can range from staging a mock mass casualty to being really lazy and going out in the ambulance for ice cream.

Between Monday nights there are work details. They are called whenever something needs doing, which can range from scrubbing the ambulance to sweeping out the fire engine bays to hauling the Christmas lights down from the attic.

I have showed up on a Saturday afternoon to help sweep out the fire bays. The engines are all pulled out, and I sensibly wear jeans and a work shirt and heavy boots. I am looking forward to hanging out with the firemen. I love firemen.

When Michael and I used to live in another Connecticut town many years ago, a batty old lady lived in the apartment above us and always fell asleep while cooking something on her stove. On a regular basis she would set off fire alarms in her house and the town fire department would race to our building to snuff out a blazing chicken breast or a scorched steak. I liked the old lady's fires because I was mad for the firemen. They were out of *Playgirl* magazine, big handsome hunks of men, wearing skintight T-shirts and yellow fire pants held up with red suspenders. They knew they looked hot and they were big flirts, casting a wink at me, flexing an arm muscle lazily as they put on their gear. I dreamed of their bunkhouse, of how spectacular it would be to sit with them at a long table and share a meal.

Now I had dozens of firemen of my own. I had seen them around town, racing to fires or washing the fire trucks in back of the firehouse, but never met them. I had admired their fire gear, the hats and jackets with their names on the back hanging on hooks, their boots and pants lined up and ready to leap into at the first call of trouble. The fire bay smelled like smoke and rubber; the huge fire trucks gleamed, the chrome polished like something in a jeweler's case.

When I arrived on Saturday morning for the work detail, a dozen firemen were already scrubbing and sweeping the bays. I was the only woman who showed up. When I appeared everyone grew silent. Only minutes before I could hear the banter, the curse words, the happy chatter; and now with me there, they acted like a nun had walked in on their fun. They swept the floors grim-faced and with eyes cast downward.

I tried to make conversation, but could think of nothing to say. We all swept in silence for an hour and then I could see a huddle forming. Someone was going out to the deli to get egg and bacon sandwiches and coffee. A fireman named Chris was taking orders and money. I kept sweeping. I didn't know what to do, I was too shy to ask them to pick something up for me. They were too shy to ask me. In the deathly quiet of the bay I heard someone mumble, "Do you think *she* wants something?"

"I dunno," said another.

They stood and looked at me sweep but no one said anything. The egg sandwich guy got in his pickup truck and drove the half mile to the deli. My stomach was rumbling by the time he came back. The guys stopped work and all got their sandwiches and steaming cups of coffee.

In silence they unwrapped their fried eggs and bacon sandwiches and started to eat. They sipped coffee. I swept. I was now standing in the middle of a semicircle of eaters. I felt my cheeks flush. I wanted to put the broom down and run away. I could feel a blister start to form on my thumb where the heavy push broom had made a groove.

I could see an extra egg sandwich and a cup of coffee in the cardboard box.

Finally one of the firemen walked up to me. The other guys looked at their feet. "There's a sannich for you and some coffee," he said.

I beamed. "Thanks, what do I owe you?"

Caught off guard, he didn't answer, instead picked up a broom and started sweeping next to me.

I looked at the guys. No one would make eye contact. I walked over and peeled the wrappings back from the sandwich. I took a swig of coffee. I never take sugar in my coffee, and this was prepared the way all the guys drink it: "regular" . . . with milk and sugar.

"Thanks," I said with a mouth full of food. No one looked up. Nothing ever tasted so good to me.

I am having an attack of "firsts." Here is what I dread and what I have yet to endure as an EMT. Top of the list are dead people. I have not yet met the dead, either cold and old ones or the new and still warm. I have not been puked on, I have not seen feces, domestic abuse, child abuse, or amputations. I run through the list in my head in the same way I would a shopping list of what to buy at the supermarket. If you are ever unlucky enough to ride in an ambulance as a patient, there are two unofficial rules you should know if you want the EMTs to like you: don't die and don't barf. The former makes us look bad, the latter makes us as sick as you.

Little do I know I am about to meet my first dead person. I forget how the call was toned out, but it didn't sound all that bad, maybe something like "Ambulance, please respond to 776 Old Borden Highway for man with loss of consciousness." I run out the door and into my car. It is broad daylight, nice and sunny, nothing creepy in the air. I drive a mile and pull into the driveway. As usual, the ambulance has already beat me there. I am without a doubt the slowest EMT in the world, although I feel I am driving so fast I am flying. I imagine flames shooting out from under my Subaru's tires.

At the bottom of the stairway is a man with a broom. He is sweeping dirt off the exterior stairs that lead up to an apartment. By the look of the scene the call is nothing much, maybe someone fainted. I tap on his shoulder. He spins around to acknowledge my presence.

He has the largest goiter I have ever seen; it practically envelops his face.

I resist my urge to freak out. He is oddly nonchalant as he sweeps. "My brother is upstairs." He points with the end of the broom. "He is not looking well."

I can see that Bernice and a bunch of firemen have already arrived on the scene, so, not to crowd them, I stay downstairs and take out my pad and start writing.

"Your brother's name, please," I ask, then scribble it down.

"Does he have any allergies?"

"When was his last meal?"

"Any medications that he is on?"

As I go down the list my attention is drawn away from the man with the goiter. I look up to see four of our biggest firemen carrying a lifeless figure down the narrow staircase on a stretcher. The man is blue-gray; he is also enormously fat, can't weigh less than 300 pounds. He is naked, and his face is damp and covered with drying Cheerios and milk.

Bernice points to the ambulance and at me. "Can you ride with us?" she asks. I jump in without thinking.

The paramedic has appeared and the CPR that was started upstairs in the man's apartment is now being continued in back of the ambulance. I am at his head. I have a plastic device called a bag valve mask in my hands. It is hooked up to the oxygen tank, and with this I force air down his throat as Bernice and the paramedic take turns doing compressions on his chest.

The dead have little dignity in the back of an ambulance, even less if they are blue, naked, fat, and covered with cereal. Between beats I have to ask Bernice, "What the hell happened?"

She is catching her breath as the paramedic does the chest compressions and I continue to bag.

"I don't know. He was this color when we got there. Looks like he has been dead for some time. He was sitting naked at the kitchen table with his face in his cereal bowl."

"Shit, this guy is huge," says the paramedic as he pushes hard on the chest.

I don't even begin to know what to ask Bernice next. I

want to know why his brother has a goiter the size of a football and why he didn't notice sooner that his sibling was blue. Where to begin? And then I am struck by the fact that not only am I sitting in the back of the ambulance but that the big head that I have clutched between my knees belongs to a DEAD person. The dead man is looking at me with his dead eyes. His pupils are fixed and dilated, the eyes themselves a blue-gray like his skin. His eyes are open; I am using both hands to "bag" him, so I can't close them. They look like the eyes of a big dead fish on display at a seafood store.

The oxygen line to the main tank slips off the end of my bag mask. I panic. "Don't worry," says the paramedic, still doing compressions. "You can't hurt him." This is a confirmation that he is truly dead, beyond our help or ability to hurt. We are just going through the motions. By law we have to continue CPR until we get him to the hospital and he is pronounced officially dead by an MD.

When this thought sinks in, I start to relax. I am so happy that his life doesn't rest in my hands that I forget that I am afraid of dead people. My experience with the dead has been very limited. The only dead person I have seen was my mother in her coffin, embalmed and poufed up with a pink chiffon turban on her bald head from where the chemotherapy had denuded her. I thought all dead people looked like that.

I had always heard that dead people smelled bad and they leaked pee and shit and their tongues lolled out. This man didn't do any of these things, at least not yet.

We ride wordlessly in the ambulance, the dead man's head in my lap. I poke at his cheek with a gloved forefinger just to see what he feels like. He feels like a human being. After we arrive at the hospital we wheel him out on the stretcher and continue doing CPR all the way to the Trauma Room, when Dr. Blasco, a slight, dour woman in a starched white coat, comes in. She takes one look at him and tells us to stop CPR. He is now officially proclaimed dead. The time is recorded.

I start to wonder if his brother is on the way to the hospital, I still want to ask about his goiter. Bernice tells me he is coming to the ER in his own car. "What's wrong with his face?" I stammer.

"Remember last year there was the call about the guy who fell down in his garage and got stuck between the washer and dryer?"

I shake my head. Bernice forgets I am new at all this.

"That was him."

"Is that how he grew the goiter?" I ask.

"No, he had it at that time, he was stuck between the washer and dryer and the firemen had to pry him out."

"Why didn't he call 911 earlier today? Why didn't he know his brother was dead when he was blue?" I ask.

I am asking the unanswerable questions. Why? Why do people live or die, or love or hate or see things or are oblivious to them?

"That was my first dead guy," I tell the paramedic, who is pulling the twelve-lead heart monitor lines off the big man's chest.

"Cool," he says, and slaps my shoulder.

In the ambulance heading back I start to feel antsy. "That was my first dead man," I tell Bernice.

"Really?" She always forgets that I have just started. "We better celebrate," she says; so we make a date to meet the next day for tea and scones with lemon curd at a "ladies' lunch" place a mile or so from the firehouse.

We sit among the potpourri and crisp lace-edged napkins and talk about the dead man. Bernice looks elegant; I am dressed up too. The waitress takes our order and is oblivious to what we mean when we say, "He went from blue to pink." She probably thinks we are talking about an interior decorator who changed a bedroom color scheme. I feel like I am in a secret society, a special club of people who know the dead, have met them personally. Now I can cross that one off my list.

10

Most people in the firehouse clutch before answering a call to the AIDS hospice, which is housed in a modest house down on Portland Avenue. The AIDS hospice is controversial. Many residents of Georgetown don't even know it is there. To others in the town its existence here is a source of great pride and it is the recipient of charity benefits. And then there are the few who think of it like a turn-of-the-century pestilence house, a place to run past and hold your breath.

Bernice has told me that as a new recruit I should not be a "first responder" there. She tells me I should wait for other people to sign on before I go. She is protecting me from walking into a scene I can't handle, and maybe she is also protecting the patients from a rookie EMT who might do something drastically wrong.

It is 2 A.M. and the tone goes off. I swim out of my sleep and write the address down on my pad next to the bed. Suddenly I remember this is the AIDS hospice, where I am not to go alone. I pull on my jumpsuit and listen for Bernice and a few others to sign on, and then I get going.

This place is also high on my list of scary things. I don't know what I will see when I get through the door. I know that our protocol is to wear not only gloves but a mask that covers the nose and mouth, and a paper gown over our clothes if the patient is vomiting or hemorrhaging. I get to the scene and find a very frightened-looking local cop standing outside. "I don't have a mask or gloves with me," he says, as if to convince me that he is better off staying outside.

"That's okay," I say. "I'll go in."

I am so used to being fearful that when I do something brave it seems almost unreal. I find that I have the capacity to worry things into the ground, to talk to Tom Knox about them until we are both beyond bored, to go into intricate relentless detail with Michael, and then—boom—out of the blue, all the fear just falls away and I am doing the undoable. I now think I am the type of person who would faint at the sight of a spider but could run into a burning building to save a baby. Fear is like a hologram. It seems filled with substance and when you go beyond it you realize it was just an illusion.

I put on my gloves and a mask. Immediately I realize that the mask is a hideous invention. It prevents me from breathing in fine particulates, but it also seems to stop 99 percent of the air, too. I feel like I am suffocating. I pull it off every few seconds to take a breath. How stupid is this; I am defeating the whole point of the mask, which I am now wearing just for show, pulling it off my face at every opportunity.

One of the night hospice workers, a stout black lady, glowers at me. "You don't need that on your face, ain't nobody in there going to hurt you," she says. I mumble something incomprehensible back at her through the mask, something about the mask being used for the protection of the patients as well as for us.

She says, "Whatever," and points me and Bernice to an upstairs bedroom. In bed is a thin black woman with wild hair. Her room at the hospice looks like a child's bedroom. It is filled with teddy bears and pictures of rainbows and balloons. It is hard to tell how old she is because she is so sick. She could be eighteen or eighty.

The stout woman hands me a computer printout of this woman's medical history, and tells us that she is to be taken to Stamford Hospital. We explain that our ambulance does not go to Stamford Hospital, just Norwalk and Danbury. This results in a debate with the hospice worker. "I guess Norwalk," she finally says, throwing up her hands. As I walk down the stairs to the ambulance I look at the patient's computer printout. She is a mess. She should be dead ten times over. She has AIDS, hepatitis, TB, thrush, and has had major brain surgery. Tonight 911 was called because she had a seizure.

She slurs when she talks, and sounds very angry. She sounds drunk, although she isn't.

"Hello, I'm Jane from the ambulance," I say.

"Fuck you," she replies.

"Are you in pain?" I ask.

"Fuck you," she says again. Can't blame her. What a stupid question. She is lying there with half a brain in her head and terminal AIDS; how could she feel anything but lousy?

"Honey," I say (I have taken to calling patients Honey or Dear, just as I was taught not to do in class, as it is disrespectful), "we are going to take you to the hospital."

Honey and Dear are handy if you suck at remembering people's names in a stressful situation. I imagine that I will be regarded with the same affection given an efficient diner waitress who calls everyone "hon."

"Ready to go to the hospital?" I say brightly, like you would ask a kid to go to the zoo.

"Fuck you," she intones rather gravely. I wonder if this is all that is left in her surgically altered brain. Maybe it is just a one-size-fits-all expression. I do not take offense.

When a patient is so sick, and yet stable, it is a long ride to the hospital because there isn't much you can do for them but try to keep them comfortable. I am riding alone with the patient in the back of the rig. Another EMT drives us to the hospital.

I turn the overhead lights on in the rig, and after I have placed an oxygen mask on her face, and comforted her as best as I am able with layers of our white woven blankets, I sit back and reread the printout that I will give to the hospital nurse. Her name is Melba Coulter and she is thirty-three years old. No previous address.

No family members. No next of kin. Her whole life as it is presented to me is just a list of medicines and symptoms and illnesses. Above the oxygen mask her crusted eyes are regarding me. She may have just come off a long seizure but there is a spark in there. I pick up her arm; it is cold and dry, thin as a Popsicle stick. I feel around for a pulse. I take a blood pressure reading. Both are low.

I go back to reading her chart. I am uncomfortable and looking for something to do, to try to make it seem like I am of some actual use. At the bottom of the chart there is one line that catches my attention: *hobbies*.

How odd, I think, but I read on. Melba's hobbies are sewing and gospel singing. I cannot sew; I can replace a shirt button, but that is all. I try to imagine this skeletal woman engaged in her hobby. What did she sew? Did she have a sewing basket at one time and a place to live and clothes to repair? Maybe she sewed quilts, maybe she sewed for a living. What happened? I wonder if she can see well enough now to thread a needle.

I know more about gospel music than I do about sewing. I love gospel music. As I look at Melba, I think of my travels through the South with Michael and how we collected many tapes and CDs of groups like the Mighty Clouds of Joy and The Dixie Hummingbirds, which we listen to in the car. My mind wanders back to a trip to Los Angeles many years ago when we ducked out of the blazing midday sun and into a darkened movie theater, where we saw the movie *Gospel,* a documentary like *Woodstock* but with black sacred church music instead of stoned white hippies. I was so moved by *Gospel* that halfway through it I had to stand up and dance in the aisle. I testified, I witnessed, I was slain in the spirit. Not bad for a New York Jew on vacation.

Now in the back of the ambulance I start humming a snatch of gospel music to myself. One of my ten wishes would be to sing like Mahalia Jackson. I can't, but it is fun to pretend. "Melba, it says here you like gospel music," I say.

I am expecting a "fuck you," but it doesn't come. Maybe I can't hear it over the swish of the oxygen mask.

"I really like Shirley Caesar," I tell her, thinking of her showstopping performance in *Gospel.* Ageless Shirley—short, powerful, and snub-nosed—pantomimes carrying the heavy cross Jesus was crucified on. She sings "No Charge," a heartbreaking song about a mother's priceless love for her ungrateful son. She jumps as if she is on a pogo stick, and wipes the sweat from her furrowed brow as she pours her soul into every word.

Melba's crusted eyes move rapidly back and forth. I wonder if she is about to have another seizure. If she does I should put on the full protective gear because she will lose control of her saliva and her bowels, and I am scared of all her diseases.

"I like her too," she says weakly beneath the oxygen mask.

I am stunned that she can speak. That she is lucid.

"My husband really likes the Clark Sisters," I say, thinking of the three robust gospel divas who have a five-octave range and enough power in their dancing to rock the house.

I wonder: before AIDS emaciated Melba, was she herself as fat and sassy as one of the Clark Sisters? I start naming gospel singers, and with each name she nods back, and I see her try to smile. The whoosh of oxygen is loud in the rig. If she is talking, I can't hear her.

I am not a singer, and I never will be Mahalia Jackson, but I try to quietly sing a few lyrics that I know from *Trouble of This World*. I have a captive audience of one. I hope the driver in the front of the ambulance doesn't hear me. It is a private thing for me to do. It is not unthinkable that Melba might die between the hospice and the hospital, that I will be the last face she sees and the last voice she hears. I want to say something meaningful to her, something more than "Where does it hurt?" So I sing secret lullabies, parts of songs. I hold her hand in my gloved hand. My mask makes it hard for her to hear me, her oxygen mask makes it hard to hear her. In movie deathbed scenes people do not wear masks and gloves, last words are whispered and heard, and all the tubes and gloves and masks of modern medicines are not intrusive.

We arrive at the hospital. It is late at night and the nurses are their usual stressed-out selves. When I first started as an EMT I took their behavior personally. They didn't smile and look happy to see me. I have come to understand that what an ER nurse or doctor must feel is the way I feel after my most exhausting ambulance ride, multiplied a dozen times over.

As we wheel Melba in on the stretcher I give some information to one of the nurses and tell her that this patient wants to go to Stamford Hospital.

"Well, why did you bring her here?" the nurse asks.

"Because Georgetown doesn't take people to Stamford," I say.

"Well, somebody will have to arrange transport for her there," she says, reading her chart.

We stand in the hall with Melba lying stiffly on the cot, all of us waiting for something to change.

"Okay, for now take her to Room 8. We will evaluate her and see if she is stable enough to send to Stamford."

I see one of the other nurses is on the phone with the hospice trying to arrange transport for her to Stamford. My fellow EMT who drove the rig has now cleaned and sanitized the ambulance while I was talking to the nurses and has come in to locate me. I can tell he wants to get going, but I still have to fill out the run form, the long and detailed paperwork that goes along with each 911 call. I see him fidget, wanting to get out of here. Melba has been taken off our ambulance stretcher and placed in one of the curtained ER rooms. She is all alone. Her eyes have retreated back in her head. I see a nurse push the curtains aside and ask her a question. I can see her mouth forming the words "fuck you" through her clear oxygen mask.

I walk over to her. I touch my hand to her shoulder blade, which juts starkly through her nightgown. " 'Bye, Melba," I say. I have taken off my mask, so she can hear me better. She fixes her eyes on me but doesn't say anything.

"Take care of yourself," I say, knowing she is unable to care for herself.

She takes one long last look at me and turns her face to the wall to wait for the next ambulance and the next ride.

By the time I climb back in the ambulance, the driver has folded all the clean blankets and sheets, rolled up the blood pressure cuff and stethoscope. It is like a fresh hotel room. There is no trace of Melba anymore.

"Let's go," I say, and we take off for home. I feel like crying but my eyes remain dry, like Melba's. *"Hobbies: sewing and gospel music,"* I repeat to myself, and turn out the overhead lights on the ceiling of the ambulance as we glide through the night toward home in darkness on a trip where someone will be happily waiting for me at the other end. I am very fortunate.

11

I am an only child and a writer by trade, both lonely situations. After my mother divorced my father, I grew up as a latchkey kid, came home from school to an empty apartment, watched TV, read, goofed around in my own fantasyland. Sometimes I made phony phone calls to strangers just to hear another voice. As an adult, life is not that different. As a writer I work at home, I don't have children. I can stay home for days in my bathrobe and no one will say anything. Even when I am not depressed it is seductive to do this. I am used to myself as my best company. I have never had to deal closely with other people on a day-to-day basis until I became an EMT. Now I have to deal with a firehouse full of people.

I always wanted to be from a big family, although I had no idea what that really meant. I pictured everyone sitting happily together at mealtimes, idyllically exchanging Christmas presents beneath a tinsel-laden tree. Now I have thirty-five brothers and sisters—my fellow

EMTs and firemen—and I am, at last, in a family of sorts.

The first thing I begin to realize about families in real life, as opposed to my TV sitcom–fueled fantasies, is that they fight with each other constantly about everything. My new firehouse family is dysfunctional, or maybe it is typical; I wouldn't be a good judge. I always dreamed about having seven brothers, and now I have many times that number. Their favorite things to do are smoke and drink, eat pizza and curse, and, of course, put out fires.

I still sense that to be a woman at the Georgetown Volunteer Fire Department is to be an interloper, and I try to make myself as near invisible as possible. Dot, who joined the department at the same time I did, feels no such compunction.

Once a month we have monthly business meetings, which I adore. I love the ritual of sitting on metal folding chairs in a big room full of macho men, most of whom smoke. We stand and salute the flag, say the Pledge of Allegiance, listen to the reading of the minutes of the last meeting, and for the next two hours, we argue with one another, name-call, are generally rotten, and at the end, when the meeting is concluded, go to the big room and drink sodas and eat candy.

What I begin to realize as I go on more calls and attend more meetings is that in a firehouse family, it is fair to say that although everyone spends a lot of time bitching and gossiping about everyone else, the truth is that most everyone would walk into a burning building to help their fellow members. Our lives depend on each other. At a fire, an accident, or a crime scene, you better know who has your back covered. This doesn't mean that cliques don't form and that people don't gossip, and at times it feels like saying hello to someone is setting a match to a keg of dynamite.

I am on my best behavior at business meetings; I want to do nothing to upset the status quo. I sit in awe of people like Eddie, an eighty-five-year-old "life member" of the department who comes to every monthly meeting in his Georgetown fire department baseball cap and smokes a huge cigar through the whole proceedings. I pointed him out to Michael once when I saw him in town and Michael said he was a dead ringer for the movie director John Ford.

We are all sitting in the meeting room when Dot raises her hand. I know trouble is coming. I know she is going to propose a change in the way things are done. The chief calls on her from the table where he and the president and the firehouse secretary sit, at the front of the room near the American flag.

Dot begins a lecture about secondhand smoke and how Eddie and the rest of the guys are putting her health at risk, how she is getting asthmatic at meetings, how her hair and clothing stink at the end of the evening.

I feel my toes curl in my shoes. How could she have

the nerve, the gall, to demand that the guys give up smoking? What will happen to Eddie? There is a deathly silence. I am afraid for her, and for me, because I don't want anything to change at this firehouse. I don't want it modernized or "improved." It is, to me, perfect the way it is.

I am expecting World War III, but it doesn't materialize. You can't fight political correctness these days, and as the guys stub out their cigarette butts and Eddie chews on the rope of his now unlit cigar, the vote passes to ban smoking at the firehouse. Eddie never comes to another meeting.

I began to see that there is a definite pecking order to life in Georgetown, and it is similar to small towns everywhere that have been discovered by yuppies and commuters from the big city.

In the four towns whose butt ends converge in Georgetown there are now many wealthy people living in the big new McMansions that sell for a million dollars and more. We have a handful of famous people, one well-known political pundit, a rock star, a famous writer, some big-name artists, and plenty of people who drive through shabby Georgetown in their Porsches and BMWs to towns with fancier zip codes.

What they don't know is that the true power brokers of the town regard them as arrivistes and nobodies. The town is run by people who have grown up here, and in many cases have forebears who were townies as far back at the 1700s.

These people do not live in the million-dollar homes or drive sports cars. Instead they pump gas at the local station, work in the grocery store, deliver oil to houses, or are plumbers and handymen and garbage truck drivers. They know everything about the town, they know where the skeletons are buried. The rich newcomers think they own the town but it is just an illusion. If you need anything done, if you need a deed to your property, or your septic tank cleaned, or an ambulance or fire rescue, you are dealing with the real owners of Georgetown.

Our fire chief and his three brothers are among the true elite. The Heibeck brothers occupy the highest positions in the firehouse. When they aren't doing firehouse duties they are pumping gas and fixing cars at the service station they own, a quarter mile away from the firehouse. They are men of few words. In fact, for the first year I serve at the firehouse our conversation never goes beyond "Hello" . . . and even that is a stretch. Usually, all I get is a nod of the head.

Michael comes home one day after having coffee with a local who knows the Heibeck brothers. He tells me this man said the Heibeck brothers like me. I am on a cloud of joy all day. I am getting in with the in crowd; I am on my way to getting "made" if I have their approval.

I remember all the years I lived in town and pulled in for gas at the Heibeck brothers' service station. Back in the 1980s, swelled with the easy money of the decade, Michael and I bought a big black Mercedes-Benz. We were among the town's new strivers, we thought the town's importance was reflected in the stockbrokers and the celebrities and the corporate types who commuted into the city. I never paid much attention to the Heibeck brothers; they were just four townies wearing mechanics' jumpsuits. They took my Visa card and swiped it when I had a full tank. We brought in our Mercedes to have the oil changed. Michael and I thought they were impressed by us.

Now when I stop at the service station my eyes are cast downward with humility. I am not humble because the Mercedes is long gone and replaced by a Subaru. I am humble because Mike Heibeck is the fire chief and I now call him Chief instead of Mike when I hand him my credit card.

I genuinely like all the Heibeck brothers. On the 1 to 10 scale of gregarious they range from a 1 to maybe a 3, but they are the best kind of good old boys: delightfully old-school when a lady is present, no cursing, no coarse behavior.

I also love thinking about how deep their knowledge of the town is.

I am called out for a 911 call to a house down the road from me. It is a conspicuously expensive house recently occupied by a Boston couple who wanted to go rural in

Connecticut. The husband of the couple, who can't be more than thirty-five, is slumped over in the bathroom, apparently from a heart attack.

The ambulance races to the scene, and I see the chief is there as well. The house is newly decorated and elaborately furnished. It bears the professional mark of a good interior designer.

"I don't know what is wrong with my husband," the wife cries. "He just collapsed. I think he is dying." I am not so sure he is dying but he looks sick enough to me; gray-faced and semiconscious.

"It smells very fumy in here, maybe it is the new floors or fresh paint," one of the EMTs says. "Maybe that's what's wrong."

We load the husband on the stretcher and wheel him out to the waiting ambulance. He is getting oxygen but lies as limp as a flounder on the cot. The chief and I exchange glances. I know exactly what he is thinking. We don't have to say a word to one another. We both know this house is cursed. Fifteen years ago there was a spectacularly gruesome murder here; the couple who lived in the house were killed by their grown son who had been institutionalized for most all his adult life. After the son killed them he chewed on them like a cannibal until he decided that he'd better leave and drove himself to Vermont, where he was soon found and brought back to stand trial in Connecticut. Since this horrible event the house has gone through many new owners, leaving behind a string of divorces, abandonments, and bankruptcies. I wonder if the new owners or the previous ones have any idea that they are sleeping in a house that comes straight out of Stephen King. It is not something most people would think to ask about when house hunting.

But even if they don't know, I know, and of course the chief knows, and we each know the other knows, and we will not tell the new people what we know. It is a town secret, the kind of thing only the true elite are privy to.

12

Every Monday night at the firehouse we have a drill. Keeping our skills fresh is a big part of being an EMT or a fireman.

The gruff man who first let me look around the ambulance has been with the fire department for forty-five years. His name is Charlie Pfhal, and he has turned out to be an amazement and an inspiration to me. He is a tough old bird, speaks his mind, will nail a liar or a bullshit artist within ten seconds. And although he is edging his way toward eighty, he still drives the ambulance and runs the EMT side of the firehouse.

He and Bernice are the driving force for the EMTs at Georgetown and they are always trying to get the name of the firehouse changed from Georgetown Fire Company to Georgetown Fire and EMS. The firemen hate this idea, they feel it disrupts the unity of the firehouse for EMTs to be separated out, and this ongoing simmering feud periodically erupts into fights, harsh words, and stubborn behavior.

You can see the tension at the Monday-night drills. The EMTs want to practice EMT things, like using the suction unit in the rig, finessing the defibrillator, wrapping wounds, and splinting fractures. The firemen want to play with their hoses, and they want us EMTs to join in the fun.

I have never seen a fire truck that doesn't gleam, and while Georgetown may have an old ambulance, its fire trucks are polished to military precision. The pride of the outfit, Tower 8, is a half-million-dollar aerial tower truck that looks like a new toy just taken out of its box.

I had no idea how labor-intensive fire equipment upkeep is. Not just the trucks get scrubbed and buffed, but every hose, every rescue rope, every ladder is gone over until it is in perfect condition and rolled, folded, or mounted exactly right on the truck.

The firemen want the EMTs to drill with them. To roll hoses and do rescues. Sometimes we EMTs do this, other times we sneak off on Monday night and do ambulance things and come back to the "barn," as the firehouse is called, to find a tangle of angry, sulky firemen rolling their hoses and looking abandoned and mad. "I will not roll hose," Bernice says. "They don't clean the ambulance or fold blankets for us, so forget about it."

My secret is that I actually like drilling with the firemen. Although I want to stay on Bernice's good side and can grumble right along with her, there is something terrific about watching the fire side work out. I have held the turgid hoses while the water blasts through it, steadied the magnum pressure against my hip. It is a heady feeling, as is going up in the basket atop the aerial truck seventy feet in the air.

I also like drilling with the firemen because it has been my observation that there is no such thing as an ugly fireman. It is amazing how even the plainest sap transforms into hunkhood the minute those outfits go on. Slack-jawed guys whom I have seen watching fishing shows or NASCAR on the big TV in the main room, or gobbling down the favorite Georgetown snack of a dozen hard-boiled eggs, look like demigods when they are wearing their bunker gear and hats.

The drill everyone dreads the most is ice water rescue. Exactly when it is scheduled for each year is kept a secret because it is generally assumed that if it were announced that a particular night was ice water rescue, no EMTs would show up. So what always happens is that we EMTs arrive wearing street clothes and are pathetically underdressed, while the fire guys in their bulky weatherproof suits are comfortable standing outside in the freezing night air. And thus continues the cycle of why EMTs hate cold water rescue drill, because we are freezing and uncomfortable.

Ice water rescue is always done in the middle of January or February when the lake behind Georgetown's defunct wire mill freezes over. The fire trucks and the ambulance are driven the half mile to the site (known as Toxic Pond to the fire guys), where we walk to the water's edge and wait for the action to begin.

I have a sneaking suspicion that a certain Monday night is going to be the drill, probably because the officers are all so vague about what will be happening that evening. I dress warmly—hat, gloves, down jacket—but it isn't enough outerwear and I am still freezing. The walk from the road to the pond's edge is a steep slope, covered with ice and snow. I am terrified that I am going to slip, slide, and fall into the lake.

Bernice literally shows me how to walk. This is Bernice's greatest gift, she is a fount of practical wisdom, something my parents were sorely lacking in. I may be exaggerating, but I can't think of a single practical thing I learned growing up except once when our housekeeper, who grew up in a shack in Alabama, told me all hangers in a closet should be in the same direction so if there was a fire you could reach in and grab your clothes in a big armful and run.

Now I am getting walking lessons. "Walk with your feet sideways and lean uphill," Bernice tells me. "Like you're skiing," she adds—making me feel like a total nerd because in my entire life I have never skied. Bernice, her husband, and her two handsome sons are all jocks.

"I don't know how to ski," I whimper as I clutch her, trying not to fall. She explains to me the logic that if your feet are pointed straight ahead that is where you will slide; if your feet are angled away from the slope, you stay put. It is amazing; I inch down the slope and I am not slipping. I can walk on ice; I feel like I am walking on water.

"Be careful at the edge," Bernice tells me. She remembers the first ice water rescue drill we were on together. I fell through the ice at the lip of the pond, crashing up to my thighs in the icy water. I was embarrassed and had to retreat to the ambulance, strip off my pants, and wrap blankets around me. This year I refuse to go near the edge of the water. I hover back. There is only a sliver of moon and it is hard to see what the firemen are doing way out in the middle of Toxic Pond. Soon my eyes grow accustomed to the night, and the ice on the bright pond silhouettes a fireman in a red diving suit. The other firemen have walked out onto the frozen pond and with axes are chopping a hole into which the red man will submerge himself. We are to rescue the red man by throwing rescue ropes to him and hauling him out of the water.

The panic and excitement of ice rescue makes me giddy. I am not alone. The firemen act goofy and frolic; one lies on the ice and acts like a seal, flapping his arms and legs and barking, while another group sings the theme song to the TV show *Flipper.*

Months before, we had the fire trucks removed from the bays and we were given the rescue ropes to practice throwing. The shortest one is fifty feet long, and all the ropes come coiled in a yellow or blue canvas bag. The bag has a handle that you grab onto to throw, and you hold a loop of rope that comes out the end of the bag in your hand, so when you make your throw you are still connected with the rope and can haul the person in.

Throwing a bag with a long rope in it seems easy. It isn't. In fact, even the male EMTs and Bernice, who is athletic and coordinated, are challenged by flinging this rope to the drowning victim. Since I will not go to the edge of the water, I have added at least an extra ten feet to my throwing distance. I stand on a slippery slope, wishing I had worn boots with cleats, and swing the rescue bag in the air to get the feel of it. "What's the big deal?" I tell myself as I swing the rescue bag back and forth.

I am given the go sign by the firemen in charge of the drill. I wind up like Catfish Hunter on the pitcher's mound and let go of the bag when I feel the surge of momentum building. I slide on the ice and fall on my ass; the bag flies in the air and comes down hard on the head of the assistant chief, who is standing in front of me. He is one of the Heibeck brothers, the one who hardly speaks at all. He glowers at me and says nothing, which speaks volumes. I struggle to my feet. Another of the firemen who is a training officer and who likes me comes to my aid. "If this was a real situation, Jane, you could stay in the ambulance warming it up, getting it ready for transport."

I am torn between wanting to run away and trying to throw the rope again. I am moonstruck by the cold, the icy air, the good-looking men in their fire outfits, the big red truck glowing under the stars. I pick up the bag and coil the rope inside it, which seems to take forever. I imagine this is real life and some kid is drowning, and I am taking fifteen minutes to rewind the rope. I finally get it back in the bag. "I'm going to throw it again," I announce. "Stand clear," an officer says, and the firemen back away from me and cover their heads. I throw the rope and it goes in a straight line. It does not bean anyone. But it lands approximately five feet in front of me, a good forty-five feet from the drowning victim. "Help me," the wet-suited fireman screams in faux panic as I madly coil the rope back in the bag.

Snot is running out of my nose and my knees have gone numb from the cold. I ask Greg Zap, one of the training officers, if he has a Kleenex.

"No," he says and rips a dried leaf off a small maple tree and hands it to me. "You can use it for toilet paper, too," he says. "That's what they do in the Boy Scouts."

I wonder if he thinks I have shit in my pants. I blow my nose in the leaf, which mostly spreads the snot around my face, and resist the urge to wipe my nose on the canvas rescue bag. "I'm throwing it again." People duck for cover. I wind up hard. I visualize, I see the rope floating right to the victim, I take a deep breath of freezing night air, and let go. The rope feeds out straight and true. It skitters to within about three feet of the man in the water. "Good job," someone says. I walk sideways up the hill like Bernice showed me how to do. I have two new primitive skills under my belt: walking and throwing. It is a great evening.

When the drill wraps up we all go back to the firehouse. One of the firemen shows us how to wash and line-dry all the rescue ropes. Each rope also has to be inspected inch by inch before it is put back in the bag.

I would be a terrible fireman: I do not have the patience to do this; I would smoosh the damp rope back in the bag and assume it would be fine. "I'm not rolling any rope," Bernice says. "No one helps us clean the ambulance." The simmering anger between fire and EMS is back on the front burner again.

When I first joined the fire department I was in awe of and uncomfortable around the firemen. One of the first times I was at the firehouse was after a large fire where a big two-story house burned to the ground. The guys had been fighting the fire for many hours before it was extinguished. The ambulance had come back to the firehouse before the fire trucks and I had gone upstairs to the ladies' room to wash my face and brush my hair. Before putting my hairbrush back in the locker I felt the building shake. The fire trucks were pulling into the bays. The guys were back. Someone, knowing they were on their way back to the firehouse, had sent out an order for a dozen pizzas from the local Italian place. The pizza boxes were stacked like magazines on the bar in the great room. The heady scent of pepperoni and sausage filled the air. I stood in the hallway. I was going to go home, but I could hear footsteps in the stairwell and knew that all the men who had just fought a fire were now coming back to replenish themselves. I opened the door to the stairwell and could hear the sound of heavy bunker boots. I could hear voices.

"Fuckin' A," someone said.

"Fuckin' fire," someone else said.

"There better be some fuckin' thing to eat up here," another voice called out.

I slipped back into the ladies' room. I didn't want to go against the tide of firemen heading upstairs. I could smell the sweat on them, the smoke and testosterone pushing the wake in which they walked. Their voices all merged into one. "Fuck, fuckety fuck, fuck you, fuck him, fuckin' shit, fuck."

"Fuckin' pizza," someone said ravenously, and when the stairwell was clear I flew downstairs and into my car. I put a Tracy Chapman CD in the player, and reached into my purse and sprayed myself with girly-type floral cologne. I needed some female juju to overcome the tidal wave of manliness that had just swept in the door.

My first big fire came on Thanksgiving Day, at two in the morning. It was an early winter that year and there was a freezing sleet already covering the branches of the trees and the road. I heard my tone go off, and that the call was for mutual aid from the surrounding towns for a "fully involved structure fire."

I missed the ambulance leaving the firehouse and drove to the scene in my own car.

The roads were slick and my car skidded at every turn.

There was no traffic on the road because of the early hour. People lay sleeping snugly in their beds, plump plucked turkeys waiting to be roasted sat in the refrigerators, feasts to be made at daybreak were about to begin.

I could smell the fire before I saw it; an acrid heavy scent blanketed the still night air. I could see the fire trucks parked up ahead, along with our ambulance. I parked my car as close to the scene as I could and began to trot toward the fire, carrying my jump kit and my oxygen tank. My feet skidded on the frozen road surface. The closer I got the noisier things became. I could hear the crackle of wood, the harsh sound of water being sprayed from the aerial truck on the flames, and I could hear the sound of four people screaming for their lives.

A family dressed only in skimpy nightclothes clung to the roof as the flames swirled toward them. Our firemen were trying to get to them, to pull them off the roof to safety. It was so cold that the water being sprayed on the roof froze on contact, leaving long icicles.

I was terrified. I had never seen a serious fire before, never smelled the black char, heard the crackle and rumble of fire eating a building from the inside out, or heard the fire chiefs screaming out orders to the men.

For a moment I stood hypnotized. I couldn't go forward, and there was a great primitive drive in me telling me to run fast, away from the danger. As the two forces battled, I stood stuck in place, wanting to move forward to help and yet wanting to get far away to safety. With a grunt of determination I started edging forward. I was well behind the fire line but I felt that the flames were going to reach out for me like a fiery hand, grab me, and pull me up to the roof. My eyes stung, I could feel the charcoal taste deep in my throat. It was cold out but the radiated heat from the fire made my face burn.

I watched as the men from Georgetown climbed ladders and fought the flames. The house, a gracious old Victorian, had fire coming from every window on every floor. Part of the roof had already collapsed, and the four people (a mother, father, and their two teenagers) screamed and swatted away embers that rained down on them.

I tried to remember everything I knew about burns, about the severity of different thicknesses, and how to use a table called the Rule of Nines, which measures the size and severity of a burn depending on where it is on the body and if it is on a child or an adult. I searched my memory for treatment of smoke inhalation, and how to use a burn blanket to cover singed flesh. My mouth was as dry as tinder as I approached the ambulance. Bernice was busy getting things inside the rig ready for the people on the roof when they were taken down. Two other ambulances from nearby towns pulled up, standing by in case any of the firemen were injured.

Firemen do not give up easily. When they start fighting a fire it is hard to tell them to stop. It is the EMTs' job to monitor their blood pressures, check for oxygen levels and exhaustion, and help make the call that tells them that they are not to go back to the fire because their health is at risk. If you do, you must prepare to be cursed at by them. They do not want to leave.

Watching our firemen battle the blaze was like watching someone voluntarily going into hell. Fire is tactile; it gets into your pores, in your hair, in your mouth; you can chew on its taste and rub it from your eyes. The closer you get, the more it paws at you, licks at you like a rough-tongued cat. Our men were right above the flames, the roof was about to collapse, and with the aerial truck they were coming in for the final attempt to pull the people off the roof.

Huddled in the basket atop the aerial truck, the family was slowly lowered down. When they hit ground level we EMTs took over. Many things beside the fire could still kill them, including hypothermia. They were nearly naked, standing wet and shivering in the winter air. We wrapped them in blankets, we checked their nose hairs to see if they were singed, we wiped their faces with sterile water, and irrigated their eyes, which were inflamed from the smoke. We gave them oxygen and transported them quickly to the hospital—two in our ambulance, two in the ambulance from another town. By the time we returned to the scene it was almost daybreak, but the fire was still raging. The house had crumbled in sections; the outer rim of walls remained, but the floors and interiors were a sick black hole in the center from which smoke still billowed forth.

I looked at our firemen, we pulled some off the scene

to check their vitals. One sounded asthmatic, another spit out charcoal-tinged sputum, another stood by the side of the ambulance and heaved vomit on his boots. Their faces were black with soot and sweat, and their fire jackets smelled like toast.

It took until noon Thanksgiving Day for the fire to be under control. There was nothing left of the house, it had burned to the ground. The four people had been given clothing to wear at the hospital and were told repeatedly how lucky they had been not to get killed.

The local paper ran a big story about the fire, and how it was started by a single candle that was not extinguished before the family went to bed. The paper showed the remains of the house, a heap of rubble behind a yellow police rope. There were the usual snapshots of the firemen, which looked like pictures of firemen you have seen a hundred times, guys with hoses spraying water on the flames. The reality of the scene didn't translate correctly to newsprint.

I took a souvenir of that fire back home with me. Jumping out of the back of the ambulance onto the asphalt road, I landed so hard I broke three bones in my right foot. My adrenaline was so high it took me until the next day to know I was injured. A bone scan at the hospital confirmed the fractures. I was given a clumsy orthopedic boot to wear and told to stay off my feet. The boot lasted six hours until I unstrapped the Velcro fasteners and threw it to the back of the closet. I took a lot of Motrin and developed an interesting hobble that slowed me down. People were respectful when I gimped toward the ambulance with my "war wound." It took a full year before I could walk without pain. But I would rather limp around on a broken foot than spend five minutes fighting a fire. It is incomprehensible how people have the bravery to do it.

13

There are nights when I hate the radio that sits by the side of the bed. It's a special police radio that is tuned to the emergency frequency that tones me out when a 911 call comes in. It looks innocuous, like a small black box or a laptop computer, but it has the power to wrench me awake at any hour of the night.

Most firehouses work in shifts. During your shift you live at the firehouse, eat with your fellow firemen, watch TV, knit, or do whatever you can do to occupy your time between calls. Georgetown is different. There aren't enough volunteers to fill a shift roster, so the alternative is a simple one; everyone is on duty all the time. As long as I am near my pager or the radio in my upstairs bedroom, or the two-way radio in the car, I can be called out.

Before I go to bed I stare at the radio and try to psyche it out, challenging it to let me sleep through the night instead of rudely pulling me awake. It sits on a round glass-topped table that has a luxuriously woven blue and white tablecloth I bought in Provence. Also on the table is a crystal and sterling silver shaker filled with talc that scents the bedsheets, and a pile of art books because I love to look at Pre-Raphaelite paintings of beautiful ivory-skinned women with flowing red hair before I go to bed. There is also an amethyst glass Victorian dish shaped like a lady's hand that holds a Catholic holy medal, given to me by a friend. All this is on my side of the bed, not Michael's side. It is my altar to calmness and femininity, to lovely gentle thoughts and shelter by a kind God. And then there is the radio.

I climb into bed, which has a fluffy duvet and thick square pillows in ruffled shams. In the winter there are flannel sheets, in the summer crisp white eyelet percale. The window is cracked open, I can hear an owl hooting outside. My house is on the top of a hill and my bedroom window is eye level with the tops of the tall trees, which creates a mystical floating effect when it's dark and the moonlight plays off the branches.

I settle into bed, but I am not calm. I may be exhausted but I am not calm. I am weary, weary of the box sounding the two long notes followed by the five short beeps that means I have to get up and get dressed and run out the door.

It takes me a while to forget about the box; sometimes I say a prayer asking that I can sleep through the night.

Some people can wake up fast. I am not one of them. When I wake up I feel older and more fragile than I do during the day. My hands shake, I always have to pee, my knees hurt, my mouth is dry. I have to locate my glasses, my watch, and my EMT jumpsuit that I lay out on a chair by the bed. Going on a call in the middle of the night is especially tricky. It is hard to know how to dress properly. Say there is an automobile accident involving an elderly person. It is winter and you might be standing out in the road for an hour or more while the person is extricated from the car. During this time you will freeze if you are not wearing layers of clothes, heavy shoes, socks, a hat, gloves, the works. But in the back of the ambulance the heat is on, and because the elderly are always cold and this one is in shock, you crank it up. As your patient is starting to feel comfortable, you are peeling off your winter wear, desperate to cool off. The back of the rig is often littered with clothes.

The worst calls are on bitter winter nights, cold stone gray ones with a freezing sheet of drizzle outside. Connecticut has a lot of these. I am in bed, in the flannel sheets, submerged up to my neck in blankets and teddy bears and sweet-smelling down pillows. The tone goes off. I bolt upright, and switch on the light to see the pad and pencil I keep next to the bed so I can scribble down the location of the call. Michael wakes up, too, groans, and buries his head under his pillow. "Turn it down," he bellows, even though I have the radio on the lowest setting. I turn off the light and try to get dressed in the dark. Michael is a very light sleeper and once he has been woken up he can't get back to sleep. At 2:30 in the morning he will trudge downstairs to make a cup of coffee as I am rushing out the door. He gives me a long-suffering look, as I mumble apologies.

I have developed tricks to make the night calls more palatable. I always grab a hit of orange juice from the fridge on the way out, so I can pump up my blood sugar. I keep my car as neat and well stocked as the ambulance so I can easily locate my rubber gloves, masks, and goggles in the dark. And then of course there are the CDs that make the transition from bed to car bearable.

I have a special collection of EMT CDs. I have chosen kick-ass Southern rock and roll for speeding along a dark road with a flashing blue light on. Black Oak Arkansas's rendition of "Jim Dandy" sets my heart pumping. Old doo-wop is great too: I sing "Rama Lama Ding Dong" as I fly around the curves. But then if I want to wallow in the whole blue muck of sickness there is Van Morrison's rendition of "TB Sheets," which gets me ready for the deathly rot that waits at the end of the driveway I'm about to pull into.

Not all night calls are bad. On a summer night it can be fun to cruise back from the hospital at 2 A.M. with the windows of the ambulance open. The breeze ruffles our light EMT windbreakers as the ambulance crew walks into McDonald's or Dunkin' Donuts with our two-way radios blathering and our stethoscopes sticking out of our pockets. The perfect sameness of fast food places is soothing. I used to think it was ghoulish to eat after a call, but now I know how much energy a call takes out of us, and this is our refueling stop. I love the cop-EMT lingo (Dunkin' Donuts is "double delta") and I love having to choose between twenty different doughnuts that all taste the same but have spangles and swirls of different-colored frostings on them.

On nights like this I go back to bed slowly, lie on top of the sheets, and think of how happy I am not to be in the hospital, to be in my own house where it smells nice and the white crisp curtains flutter on the window.

At Georgetown we are issued EMT jackets when we join. About six months after I joined the fire department, the old jackets were supplemented with state-of-the-art new jackets that form a pathogen barrier between the wearer and any icky stuff coming from a patient. The jackets are expensive; the firehouse paid around $400 apiece for them. They are rubbery on the outside and the inside has a thick thermal liner. I am beyond excitement when I get my new jacket from Bernice, but after wearing it for a few days I revert to my old limp rag of a jacket. It takes only a short time for me to realize the new jackets are hell for menopausal women like me, veritable sweatboxes with arms and a hood. They let no pathogens in, but they also let no air in, and with each hot flash I feel like I am suffocating. Dot has also gotten herself into a snit about the new jackets. It is a man's size, and the arms hang down to her knees. She complains to Bernice about the jacket, and Bernice throws up her hands. She tells Dot that she can't order anything with shorter arms, Dot does not want to pay for alterations, and the sweat-inducing expensive blue thing is flung back and forth between them like a hot potato.

Of course, one of the great things about Georgetown is how lax the dress code is. We are encouraged to wear the new blue jackets to look professional and keep ourselves safe from germs, but what we wear under them is what we happen to be wearing at the time of the call. I have answered calls in the flamenco costume I wear to my weekly dance class, and in a velvet evening dress and good jewelry. I have answered many calls in my pajamas, over which I have thrown a jumpsuit.

Sartorially, the strangest calls are the ones that take place on Halloween, the night of the Volunteer Fire Department's annual Haunted House. This event is pure Georgetown, homespun to the hilt. The point of the haunted house is to scare the local kids and then give them a bag of candy. There are other haunted houses in the area, some of them genuinely scary with big budgets for special effects and illusions of smoke and mirrors. About seven miles from Georgetown there is one run by a local produce market that is so intense that grown-ups have been known to faint while inside. It features lifelike "lunatics" who run after you in the dark with chainsaws.

Our haunted house is held in one of the fire engine bays. We cordon off the area with black-painted plywood panels and curtains made of sheets of heavy black plastic. The scariest thing about our haunted house is walking through the door into semidarkness, but what you see, once inside, is pretty tame.

The first thing you will see is Nancy Davis, a pretty blond EMT with a pert nose, dressed as a witch. Even with a fake wart glued to her green-painted skin, she still looks like a preppy cheerleader. Then you get to Bernice and me. Her specialty is to dress as a mummy. I spend half an hour with her before the haunted house wrapping her in gauze bandages, then we throw some fake blood on for effect.

My costumes are more conceptual. One year I was a dead Viking, with a face painted gray-blue and a Viking helmet complete with horns. I looked more like a sickly Wagnerian opera singer than a spook. The next year I was a pumpkin-faced spider woman decked out in orange face paint and a black beret with a huge hairy fake spider sewed on the top. Neither Bernice or I look the slightest bit scary. Bernice, the former model, looks hopelessly chic even dressed as a bloody mummy.

Halloween has always been my favorite holiday. My birthday falls a few days before it, and as a child I always had an orange- and black-frosted birthday cake. What I liked about Halloween was that it was one day out of the year when everyone was supposed to be afraid. It made me feel like I had lots of company. The dark cloud of fear under which I lived, filled with ghosts of parental misdeeds, divorces, and loneliness, was mirrored back at me by images of skeletons and gravestones and monsters coming out of their graves. On October 31, the whole world jumped at the sound of footsteps on the staircase, and a thumping heart was the norm.

Bernice and I stand together and for four hours go "woooooooo" or "booooooooo" as people walk by us, and we move our hands like talons to try to look scary. We chase little kids around and really turn on the juice for smug teenagers who come in and make us feel like middle-aged soccer moms in cheap costumes. What is in the back of our minds is that if a 911 call comes in we must abandon our post at the haunted house. We will rip off as much of our costumes as we can, but it is more than possible that we will still have semipainted faces or be covered in fake blood. We always hope that we will not get a psychiatric patient that night who will see monsters jumping out the back of the ambulance to get him.

I find it comforting that the Georgetown Haunted House is so low-tech. I wouldn't admit this to Bernice, but I would be too scared to go into a haunted house that I had not seen constructed from scratch. I have to know where the exits are and what lies around each corner. Knowledge replaces terror for me, and instead of being afraid I can now safely watch one of the Heibeck brothers' young sons lying on a table, covered with raw chicken livers, screaming as if he is having live surgery performed on him. I love seeing our shy and modest chief walking around as the straw man from *The Wizard of Oz,* giving candy to little kids. I love hearing the very tidy and sanitation-conscious Bernice complain that the tub we have set out for the tiny tots to bob for apples is hideously unsanitary—"a real pathogen menace," she concludes.

Maybe most of all I love watching Mark Svenson, one of our firemen-EMTs, and the assistant chief of the department, dressed as a magician and doing card tricks and waving his magic wand for the little kids in the adjoining room where they bob for apples. Mark is gentle, kind, and brave, a family man with children of his own. Mark is also battling a life-threatening illness that slowly disables him despite chemotherapy and other heavy curatives. This is scarier than any illusion in any haunted house. I want Mark to wave his wand and make his disease go away. The kids giggle as he swoops his black shiny cape and tips his top hat at them. Tonight magic rules. Fake blood is easier to control than the real stuff. We are masters of what is scary within the walls of the haunted house. We can start it and we can stop it, unlike out there, when the tone goes off and real life takes hold.

14

The worst calls are for sick or dying children. When the tone goes off and the dispatcher gives that message, we all race out the door extra fast.

It is late spring and Georgetown proper and the four surrounding towns that we cover have started to wake up from the long winter hibernation. Gas grills have been wheeled out on decks, pool covers removed, lawn furniture taken from the garage and sponged off. Mud season, what New Englanders call the mucky months, March and April, has dried up and the buds of the trees have begun to form bright green leaves. It is a pretty time, but not when 911 suddenly sends you out to an address where a child has drowned.

Drowning itself is a weird thing. If we get to you in time, with the right kind of maneuvers and chest compressions we can get the water out of your lungs and get you breathing again. If you drown in freezing water it has an insulating effect, sending you into a frozen stupor where you still might be able to be brought back to life. The EMT motto is, you are not dead until you are warm and dead, meaning if you are pulled out of a frozen pond with a body temperature of 89, we will keep working on you until you warm to room temperature. At that point, if you still insist on being dead, well, we can't help you.

The tone goes off. The announcement that follows is grim. "Baby found floating facedown in swimming pool."

I have been sitting at the typewriter, working on a column for *Gourmet.* When I hear what the call is for, I don't waste time. I know the road this call is on, so I do not have to look at the map. I plug my blue lights in and I am flying. I don't need music to get the adrenaline going; a baby floating facedown in a swimming pool is enough to set every fiber of my body on code blue.

When I get to the address I see that the ambulance has arrived a few minutes before me. I jump out of my car, grab my jump kit filled with lifesaving tools, and run to the side of the house where I see Bernice and a few of the firemen. They are standing around looking rather annoyed. I cannot imagine what has happened. This is the kind of call that sets us all into high gear, and nobody is moving. Breathlessly I run up to them. "Where's the kid?" I ask. One of the guys flicks an index finger over his shoulder and points to a big damp lump covered with a blanket. Whatever it is is obviously wet and dead. If it is a baby, it is the biggest baby in the world. From inside the house I hear a man's high-pitched wails. He is howling like someone whose baby has just perished. I don't get it. I walk over to the lifeless mass and take a deep breath. I peel the blankets back carefully. I am afraid of what I will see. I have steeled myself to see a dead child. The first thing I see is a huge black nose. I peel the sheet back farther and I see wet fur and two big ears. I lift the blanket off and see a gigantic dead Great Dane. The dog must weigh 175 pounds dry.

"My babbbbbyyyyyyy," comes the howling from inside the house.

"What the hell?" I ask Bernice, who is collecting her things, ready to drive the ambulance home.

"He called 911 and said his baby was floating lifeless in the swimming pool and that is the way it was dispatched. His baby is a dog, and it fell in the pool and probably had a heart attack. The firefighters fished it out, but we can't take it away; we can't put that thing in the ambulance."

Bernice and the firemen on call today are not animal people. They don't understand that this huge dead dog was his baby. I own big dogs, too, and, not having children of my own, I cannot imagine any greater or more maternal feeling than I have for them. "Let me go up and talk to him," I say as they load the ambulance and pull out of the driveway back to the firehouse. I walk into the house and see a distraught man with carefully plucked eyebrows wearing a caftan. The house smells heavily of potpourri and I see a small replica of Michelangelo's *David* on the coffee table.

There is now another car on the scene. It belongs to Alice, the town dog warden. Alice is a gruff lady with hair styled like a 1950s hoodlum. She knows I like animals and we have always gotten along. She is trying to comfort the hysterical man, who has now doubled the wallop of his grief by thinking about what his live-in boyfriend will do when he comes home in the evening from work.

"Ruffers was his baby, too," he caterwauls. "He will kill me when he sees what happened."

The police are on the scene and the dog's owner falls onto a blue-fronted chest, crying hysterically. The cop pries him loose and asks him if he has anyone he can call so he isn't alone. He gives a phone number. I call it and almost instantly the next-door neighbor comes running over with her four-year-old in tow. The child becomes upset by the apparent stress of the scene and starts crying too.

The cop asks Alice and me "where the victim is."

"The dead dog?" I say, reminding him that this is not a homicide. We point to the lump outside under the blanket.

We leave the cop behind with the owner, who is still crying and wringing his hands and explaining that his boyfriend will go ballistic when he finds out the dog died under his watch. "Can you help me transport it?" Alice asks me. "I have a stretcher in the back of my van." I walk to the van with her and she pulls out a two-foot metal stretcher that maybe would accommodate a beagle.

"Hmmm," we say in unison, and realize the only way we are going to get the dog into the van is by carrying it. Wet, we estimate it weighs close to 200 pounds. It is truly dead weight and it is also slippery.

We don't want the owner to see us dragging the dog across the lawn by its hind legs, its head hitting rocks, and now the four-year-old neighbor has wandered out to watch what we are doing.

"Go inside, little girl," I say.

"No," she says, and stands watching us.

"It's up to us," I say, and Alice nods in agreement.

She picks up the dog's head. I get his back end, the sheet begins to slip off, his big pink tongue lolls out.

"Nice doggie," the toddler says.

By inches we creep to the back of the van. It takes twenty minutes of slowly walking, putting the dog down, getting our breath back, and starting again until we get there. We open the van's hatchback and realize that there is not enough room for the dog. It is filled with all manner of lead lines and collars and the mess of dog warden paraphernalia.

We spend another twenty minutes moving Alice's canine control tools into the back of my car. We make room for the dog and, on a count of three, we manage to hoist him into the back of the van.

The four-year-old has watched our every step. "What's wrong with the doggie?" she asks.

"He's asleep," I say at the same time Alice says, "He's dead." The kid seems oblivious to both answers.

Once we stuff the dog in the back of the van, Alice says, "Meet me at the Georgetown Animal Hospital."

By the time we get there, Alice has called ahead and two vet tech assistants with a large metal stretcher on wheels are waiting to take the dog inside through the back door. They deposit the dog on the surgical table without the sheet and I see how nice he is. I can imagine becoming very attached to this dog when he was alive. I pet his lifeless head. "Good boy," I mutter under my breath. "All dogs go to heaven," I add. I hope this is true. It is what I would want for my "babies."

I never knew when I became an EMT that I would be called on to rescue a dead dog, but I am grateful that it happened. I wish I could have saved him. It would not be covered by any practice laws or EMT books, but I would have slept better at night. In my secret heart I am an EMT to all creatures.

15

One of the calls that really scares EMTs is a tone-out for a CI, which is radioese for a crisis intervention. Usually this means someone has gone crazy and needs to be transported to the hospital, and to be committed. The cops are always on scene at a CI, and the EMTs don't go in until there is someone with a gun there to protect us. In EMT class, mental illness was always discussed with a gothic "they," as if the crazy person were not only a whole other species but likely to take the EMT out with them. We were warned never to get physically close to a crazy person, lest they attack. "Watch for people who sit at the edge of the bed when you enter their room, they are likely to spring at you." Unlike sick people who have all their marbles, crazy people are not usually shown much hand-holding or compassion. If a crazy person continues to act really crazy and puts up a fuss about going to the hospital, the cops come in and handcuff him and ride along in the back of the ambulance with their guns ready in their holsters.

Coming from a family of nutty civilians and psychiatrists, I was predisposed to have more empathy for the average lunatic than many of my fellow EMTs. For me CIs are very good calls to go on. They are interesting and I know I can be of help. Somehow I know I will have the right thing to say, that I will be soothing and kind.

Unlike meeting my first dead person, which I dreaded, I was rather thrilled at the idea of meeting the town's insane folks.

When my first CI call comes over the radio, I drive with such wild abandon to the scene that the first thing I do on arrival is to smash bumpers with one of the cop cars. He glares at me. "Very nice," he says sarcastically, and then I walk by him into the building. It is a bright Sunday afternoon, and there are a huge number of people who have turned out for the call. There have to be fifteen people on scene, mostly firemen and police. To find the patient I have to make my way through a wall of firemen and police. "We have enough people upstairs," one of the firemen says to me as I attempt to push by him. I loiter around for about ten minutes and can see the exasperated looks on the faces of the cops and firemen. "What's taking so damn long?" they say to each other. "Just throw her in the rig and let's go."

"Her?" I have my opening. Women EMTs are often called on to deal with women patients and I know Bernice is already upstairs with the woman. I am the only other woman on scene. "Let me in." I push my way through. "This is a woman thing," I say. I know this is a call that I have to go on; I no longer want to run away from the ambulance.

The house sits in a desolate wooded area of Ridgefield that Georgetown covers. It is an unusual house, set way back from the road, large stone lions guarding the front door. The inside of the house is very Addams Family chic in its dark and shabby disarray. There is a suit of armor against one wall, portraits of severe-looking New Englanders on another wall. The walls are painted a deep bloodlike maroon.

I push past six foot six fireman Sean Morris, which is like shoving aside a mastiff guarding an estate gate, and walk up a narrow flight of stairs, and then down a dark hall. The macabre atmosphere inside the house sets my nerves on edge. What kind of crazy person could be waiting in her lair down the hall? I have never seen the cops and firemen look so uncomfortable. I can hear Bernice's voice coming from a bedroom. I gently knock on the door and enter, prepared to face a demon.

The CI is an ethereal young woman who looks like she weighs about 100 pounds. Long tendrils of ebony curls reach to her waist. She is wearing a thin blue silk nightgown and I can see goose bumps on her arms. She looks very frail and very cold, sitting on the edge of the bathtub in the bathroom. Mostly she looks terribly sad.

"Hi," I mutter, and look to Bernice to fill me in, give me a clue what she needs me to do.

"This is Rebecca," Bernice says in a soft voice. "She is not feeling very well, and we think it is a good idea that she go to the hospital and talk to somebody."

Rebecca, perched on the edge of the tub, has no weapon, and unless she is going to stab us with her toothbrush I see nothing around that looks dangerous.

Rebecca's husband walks into the room. He is at least thirty years older than she is; his head is covered with a wild shock of orange-red hair. He is in a heavy sweat, red in the face. "Becca, I want you to go with them *now*!" he says. His words make her cringe.

I get up and walk him to the door. I don't like the way he looks. "Do you feel all right?" I ask him.

"*No,*" he says. "I do not."

I whip out the blood pressure cuff and my stethoscope from my jacket pocket, take his arm, and pump up the black rubber bulb. His blood pressure is 190 over 110. "Why don't you sit down?" I say. "Is your blood pressure always high?"

"Yes," he says curtly, the inference being that life with Rebecca would make anyone ill.

From the corner of my eye I can see our assistant fire chief, Marty Heibeck. In the crook of his arm he holds a tiny baby. He is attempting to jiggle it to sleep as it rests on his thick muscular bicep. With his buzz-cut hair, thick wrists, and gray mechanic's pants, he looks nothing like Mary Poppins.

I walk into the nursery where he is standing. He looks wildly relieved to see me, and hands me the baby.

"Cute!!!" he says. The Heibeck brothers have perfected the art of the one-word sentence.

From Marty I learn what has happened. The baby was Rebecca's first child. During the cesarean delivery she suffered a small stroke. When poor Rebecca was released from the hospital two weeks later she went into a serious bout of postpartum psychosis. She called 911 today because she is convinced her husband is trying to kill the baby.

"Knife," Marty indicates to me when I ask how she thought her husband was going to kill it.

Poor Rebecca is so stressed out physically and mentally that she has lost the ability to differentiate truth from fantasy. Once the cops determine that her husband is not trying to kill the baby and realize that Rebecca has crossed the line of sanity, the ambulance is called to take her to the hospital.

The baby I am holding is asleep. I place him gently back on his bed.

Marty strokes the red fuzzy hair with his thick thumb, stained dark with motor oil.

"I'm going back in the room with Bernice," I tell him.

Rebecca is still sitting on the edge of the tub. The cops and firemen are getting antsy. They want her handcuffed and forced into the ambulance. Bernice and I want to finesse the situation; we want her to walk willingly with us out to the rig.

The negotiations start. "I need a sweater," Rebecca demands.

We agree that this makes sense. I go to the closet and find one and hand it to her.

"I can't leave the baby alone," she says, pointing out to the hallway, where she imagines her husband is waiting for her to leave.

"Marty Heibeck is watching your baby, he is rocking him to sleep," I say.

"You know Marty," Bernice says. "From Heibeck's Garage? Everyone knows Marty."

"Yes," Rebecca says contemplatively. "I know who he is."

Marty Heibeck is the man everyone in the community calls on for any crisis that requires brute strength. As wide as he is tall, solid brawn, Marty is exactly who you would want guarding your baby if you believed he was in danger.

"You can't leave my husband alone with the baby, do you understand?" she says again.

"Your husband will be coming to the hospital with you. The baby will stay here, and we will call a neighbor or a friend and have them come over and watch the baby," Bernice says, continuing the negotiations.

"I don't want him in the ambulance with me," Rebecca says.

"Then he will follow behind you in your car," I say.

"No good, what if he sneaks back to the house and kills the baby?"

"That is why Marty is here," I say.

While impatient cop feet shuffle in the hallway,

Bernice and I go around in illogical circles until slowly Rebecca stands up from the tub. She is so weak she clutches the wall as she rises.

Bernice helps her on with her sweater. "There, now," she says. "Let's go downstairs and take a ride to the hospital."

"Don't let him see me leave," she says about her husband.

I walk out first, take her husband by the shoulder, and lead him into another room and close the door.

"I want to take another blood pressure reading on you," I say.

"You do know she is insane," he says.

"Do you have any heart problems?" I ask.

"Angina," he replies.

"Are you having chest pains now?" I ask.

"Yes," he says. His blood pressure is even higher than before.

"Why don't you let us call a second ambulance and we will have you taken to the hospital as well," I say.

He is adamant that this is not going to happen.

"When you get to the hospital, tell the doctor what your blood pressure reading is," I tell him, writing it down on a slip of paper.

"Let's go!" I hear one of the firemen's voices call out. Bernice has successfully gotten Rebecca to walk on her own, unhandcuffed, down the stairs and into the ambulance. Lying on the cot, with her hair streaming out in waves, she reminds me of the tragic and beautiful Ophelia, decimated by mental anguish.

Bernice and one of the cops are in the back of the rig. I go back into the house. It is suddenly very still and empty. I walk up the stairs and see Marty holding the baby.

"A friend is coming over from next door in a few minutes," I tell him.

He looks relieved. He bounces the baby and strokes its head. "Cute," he says again.

"Very cute," I sigh. For a moment I imagine that I am married to Marty Heibeck and this is our house and this is our baby. It is the kind of weird intimacy that comes with the EMT job. Suddenly you find yourself in someone else's house, in their private quarters, holding their babies, looking at their stuff.

Mr. and Mrs. Marty Heibeck and family, I think to myself. Of course I would instantly redecorate the living room.

"See ya later, Marty," I say, breaking off the fantasy and letting myself out the front door.

" 'Bye," he says.

I look at my bumper, which has a good ding from the cop car I hit when I arrived. I drive home thinking about the baby. Will anyone ever tell him what happened to his mother when he was newly born? Or will this episode be expunged from the family history? Family secrets scare me. When I was a kid the odd behavior of my relatives was always whispered under the breath. No one ever came out and said, "Grandma really is insane." One relative who committed suicide was referred to so obliquely that in my childish imagination I took all the references to his "leaving a family behind" and "acting very unusual" and imagined he had run away and joined the circus. When I was thirty-five I found the "baby book" my mother had kept about my birth and formative years. It was not neatly scrapbooked but haphazardly crammed with dozens of greeting cards, letters from doctors, and notes about medications that made it quite obvious to me that my own birth had been fraught with maternal depression.

I see my mother's strange left-slanted handwriting in the book. Under "Baby's First Week" she wrote about me, "cries all the time." I can feel my mother's desperate coming apart after my birth by looking at the words. I was her first and last child. Back when I was born women didn't talk about being terrified and unhappy after a child was born.

I am more shaken than I realize by the CI. Tom Knox listens gently and when I get up from the couch to leave, in tears, he puts a reassuring hand on my shoulder. Tom often refers to the psychiatrist Harry Stack Sullivan, who postulated that craziness is not an us versus them thing, but instead places all people, from the sanest to the craziest, on a continuum. Mental illness is shades of gray. But after a really bad call I want to detach myself from craziness, get as far away as possible. I want to live only in the pure unsullied white. Gray seems dangerous, it slips too easily into black.

16

The worst crisis intervention calls are for suicides; even worse are the failed suicides—people who drink drain cleaner or overdose on pills or shoot half their heads off. Sometimes we catch them before they die; sometimes it is too late.

Once I was called to a house late at night. The estranged husband of a woman had been calling his wife's home for two days and couldn't get an answer. He finally called the police. The police called us. When we got there the woman was five days dead. She had started to decompose. She looked like she was made of melting saddle leather. The house was a mess, the physical embodiment of depression. On the mirror in the bathroom in red lipstick she had drawn a happy face, and underneath scrawled *"See you on the other side."* It made me sick to my stomach.

It is not just the dead whose tableaux stick in my mind. Sick people's rooms and the smell of them seep into my clothes and burn an image into my brain.

The world of the very sick is a deceptively cozy one, sort of like a nightmare nursery for grown-ups. Sick people wear robes that are pink and fuzzy, greeting cards and flowers line their dresser tops. But instead of the nursery smell of a freshly washed baby there is the smell of used bedsheets, of medicines, of worry.

When we arrive at the house of a sick person we are often led to the bedroom. If the patient is very sick, possibly dying of cancer or maybe ALS (Lou Gehrig's disease), they are often in a hospital bed placed in the living room, the centerpiece around which all life revolves.

Sickrooms tend to be extremely messy or extremely neat. The messy ones boast piles of magazines, books strewn about, volcanoes of pill bottles, sick-person things like spoons coated with sticky medicines and old pajamas piled on a chair. But the tidy rooms are no less unsettling. Many houses have the sick person in bed in a blank room with a religious icon above the bed and maybe a clock radio for comfort. It is hard to imagine how boring it would be to spend any time in this room, blank and lonely as a grave.

When we go to a sick person's house we ask to see all the medicines a person is taking. People either have medicines strewn everywhere or they have no idea what or where their medicines are.

On one extreme are the caretakers who not only have all their ward's medicine bottles lined up like little soldiers in a row, but have computer printouts on hand of exactly what and how much of it the sick person is taking.

The other extreme are the people who tell you, "I take a pink pill for my heart and a green one for my liver." They have no idea what the medicines are, just that they came from a doctor and are expensive.

In a third category are people whose medicines are homegrown. You would be surprised in these days of alternative health practices what weird stuff people ingest in an effort to cure themselves.

I am toned out to a pretty pink house with white shutters and a white picket fence in Redding. Bernice has already beaten me to the call. This time is different than others because the ambulance has already left with the patient, leaving Bernice behind.

"In here," Bernice calls for me when she hears my footsteps, and motions to a bedroom off a narrow hallway. There is a strange stench coming from the room. Not the now familiar smell of a sick person, or soiled underpants or layers of room deodorizer covering pee-soaked bedding that we so often gag on. This is a musty new odor, like sweat socks or damp old shoes. My eye is drawn to the top of her bureau, where there are Mason jars filled with brown fungus and what looks like malevolent toadstools. Hideous-looking warty growths flourish in the mini terrariums. In a pan is a huge fungus, like the top of a mushroom, soaking in water.

I look around the bedroom. I go into the adjoining bathroom. Unlike its prim exterior, the inside is messy, with magazines strewn about. I look at the selection of magazines. They are all related to herbal remedies and natural foods. I have heard of *Prevention,* but the other ones are obscure and new to me.

"What the hell happened?" I ask.

"As best as I can figure, the lady who lives here was trying to treat herself for something and she has been taking herbs and things. She obviously took too much or mixed the wrong things together. I don't know what she took; she was comatose when we got here." Bernice points to the big fungus in the pool of water. "See if you can find a container and let's bring it to the hospital."

I go into the kitchen and look for a Tupperware container, but I can't find one. I can't find any containers or plastic bags. There are ecological brown paper bags, but I can't use those. I find a cooking fork, big, with two long prongs. I go back into the bedroom and stand above the huge brown floating fungus. Is it alive? I am scared of it. Am I imagining it is pulsating? I can't stand the thought of touching it, much less imagine eating this nasty-looking wad of goo.

There is a small plastic wastebasket in the corner of the room. I pick it up and shake out the Kleenex and whatever else is in it. I stick the fork through the brown glob. It breaks in half; I see its underside has gills. It appears to be a giant mushroom. I stab at it again. I think of the movie *Alien,* where the scary thing flies in the guy's face and slithers down his throat. Instinctively I use my other hand to cover my lower face. I finally get a good hunk of the thing on the fork and slide it into the wastebasket.

"So you think it was an overdose of this?" I ask Bernice, pointing to the brown thing sloshing about in the wastebasket. I am terrified it is going to fall over. I steady it with my hand.

"That, or she combined it with something," Bernice says.

We carefully place the wastebasket in the back of my car, open all the windows, and drive to the hospital.

EMTs love arriving at the ER with something unusual. If you bring in someone who has a stomachache or has twisted his ankle you will probably not be acknowledged with eye contact by the staff. They will take your paperwork and get the stats from you and that's it, but the stench of what we have brought in the wastebasket already has their attention. The stink is slowly filling the ER, overpowering the medicinal smell of the hospital.

"We think the patient that arrived here about half an hour ago in the Georgetown ambulance ate some of this," Bernice tells the nurse.

The nurse looks into the pail and looks up at me. "You're kidding," she says. I shrug. I can tell she is impressed.

"I don't think I'm ever going to the health food store again," Bernice says as we walk outside the hospital to my car. Before we climb inside Bernice takes out a bottle of cologne from her purse and gives a few blasts inside my car. The stink seems to be growing exponentially. I think of the *Seinfeld* episode where Jerry's car takes on a bad smell, which cannot be removed, from a stinky valet parking guy. When I get home I pull out some "miracle" product that I bought from a late-night TV ad. I mix up a bucket of it and scrub the inside of my car with a stiff brush. In the morning it smells normal.

17

The first day I attended the class that would turn me into an EMT, each student was called upon to stand up, face the class, and tell all assembled why he or she had chosen to take the training. I remember saying that when a bad situation happened at home or on a highway, I felt like I wanted to help but didn't know what to do. I was not alone. Many people in the class expressed the same sentiments about being unable to cope effectively with emergencies, and wanting that to change. Like me, they wanted to be master of the sudden crisis, to control chaos.

I think back to the moment on the plane that was stuck on the runway and how I felt utterly powerless. All I could do was wait, like a dog with its head cocked waiting for the master's voice, for someone in the control tower to give the go-ahead to the mystery pilot behind the captain's closed cockpit. Then and only then would the plane move. Only then would I be all right.

I fought hard against the very concept of being powerless. Michael was so much more evolved than I was in this regard. An alcoholic, he had stopped drinking and had been sober for two years. He talked to me about his AA group and the twelve steps. Number one was admitting you were powerless. I hated the first step and could see no purpose in it. Fine if he wanted to relinquish trying to be the boss of things, but I, for one, was sure that if I tried hard enough I could even get planes to move on the runway.

Michael's hobby is riding horses, a high-risk endeavor. Many times, especially at night, I imagined him thrown off his horse, lying alone, somewhere in the deep woods, and no one to help him. "You must carry a cell phone," I urged. "You must carry an all-purpose knife to cut the reins or your clothes if you need to. . . . Wear a helmet," I implored. Occasionally if Michael came home with stories of his horse acting wild, my eyes would grow to saucer size and I would command, "Sell the horse. It is the only sensible thing to do." Of course, the more I complained, the faster Michael rode his horse, just as every time I explained in graphic detail the hideous things that happen in a car wreck, the faster he drove. Michael did as he pleased. I was powerless over his behavior. My trying to control him made him more reckless. Not that my suggestions were bad, but I made it clear that I felt I was in charge of keeping Michael safe and alive. Being an EMT made me even more of a control freak. I had an advanced CPR card in my wallet that declared me a "professional rescuer," and I believed my own press.

It took a personal crisis to make me realize that even with the best of help, bad things can happen to good people. We are all powerless.

The man who owned the barn where we boarded our horses was a father figure to us. Michael and I adored John, sixty-nine years old and still working twelve-hour days, shoeing horses and hauling hay. He was our fount of knowledge about horses and also about people. As a horse trader, he could psyche out a weakling or a phony right away. He was a rare thing, a real Connecticut cowboy. He dressed like a working cowboy, in Wranglers, boots, and Carhartt barn coats, and had ridden the East Coast rodeo circuit. He was rumored to be a good trick rider in his younger days.

John was tireless, although he seemed to live on a diet of Johnny Walker Black Label scotch, coffee from the nearby 7-Eleven, and Copenhagen chewing tobacco. He must have eaten, but none of us ever caught him in the act. He felt so much like family that Michael and I used to save up our frequent flyer miles and once a year we would take him with us out West, to see the real ranges and prairies that he had only heard of or seen in movies. More horse than man, he amused us with his equine-eyed travelogues. He hated the bare desert of southern Arizona: "Not a tree to stand under or any water," he said. He didn't like the trails of rocky Oregon: "Lose too many horseshoes," he grumbled. But he was enraptured with the bounty of hay he saw being harvested in Washington State. "Now that's pretty," he said with a sigh.

Then one night when he was at his horse barn, cleaning out stalls at the end of a long workday, his brain hemorrhaged and he lay at the bottom of a flight of stairs for hours bleeding intercranially until someone found him.

The EMTs were called, not Georgetown's but those of the town where he lived, and they came to get him. They did a good job because they got him to the hospital alive and in time for the neurosurgeons to operate on him and stop the bleeding in his brain.

The day after this incident Michael and I went to the hospital to see John. His head was shaved and bandaged, his arms still tanned from the late-summer sun, his muscles still bulging from a lifetime of hard physical labor.

It took two weeks for John to come out of his coma, and then the damage was assessed. His left side is paralyzed, he needs to be fed with a tube, his memory is gone. He doesn't remember he likes Copenhagen chewing tobacco or the rodeo, or pretty blondes with long legs, or balanced ride saddles from Colorado. "Saved" by the quick-thinking EMTs in the ambulance, he had gone from the master of his horsey domain to a cripple who will never be able to rise up on his own two legs from a nursing home bed.

I wear my EMT jacket to the hospital to visit him the

day after the stroke. It is protection for me, a security blanket that gives me the illusion that I have some control over this bleak situation. I am, after all, "Ambulance Girl"—invincible, like Wonder Woman in a flowing cape and tights. Of all the people on the planet, John is the last one who should have wound up as a lifelong invalid. Of course, there is nothing I can do but stand by the bedside and stroke his callused hand.

Months pass. John lies being tube fed in a hospital bed. His arms and legs atrophy and his once tan body turns a sickly shade of white. He has open bedsores and a sour smell comes from his mouth and his adult diaper. He is too messed up and weak to work the TV remote control.

After John's stroke I am thrown back into a depression and a crisis. To my dismay I no longer want to go on EMT calls. I no longer feel I am helping people to live, but rather I am intervening and not allowing them to die when it is their time. I am sure that the EMTs who came to John's rescue did the best job they could and went home feeling that they had another "save" under their belts. But I saw what was left of him after they turned the tables on his death. I prayed I would never leave anyone in that terrible state between death and life.

After John's stroke I am so deeply spooked that I don't share my feelings with Bernice or anyone else. When the tone goes off I ignore it, make a hundred excuses for why I can't go. I grow lonely and despondent, sitting once again at home in the dreaded blue bathrobe. I occupy myself by wasting lots of time, watching TV and playing around on the computer. I become an eBay geek, staying up all night logging on to auctions and trawling my favorite categories for hidden treasures that I don't need and can't afford. I go to the local discount beauty store and spend a small fortune on all sorts of facial masques and hair treatments, so when the tone goes off I am well greased and wearing a heating cap, or have drying blue clay on my face. Obviously I can't leave the house this way.

Personally things are going south fast, too. EMT, which started out as a hobby, has changed my life drastically. It has pulled me up out of a midlife funk and cast me back into a vibrant world. Now, because of what happened to John, I don't trust the magic anymore. I haunt the familiar shadows of despair. It is August and Tom Knox and his family are going on vacation. "Have a shitty time," I say as a parting farewell. He gives me the "we will have a lot to talk about in September" look as I push out the door.

August rolls into September. John is now in a nursing home. Someone has a picture of his stallion taped up above his bed. He was the only person who could ride this wild horse, and now he can't even stand up. "That's his horse," I tell one of the attendants who is cleaning him up. They could not care less. What he was before being here is of no interest to them.

Tom Knox ups my antidepressant medication. It

makes me feel marginally better, although l am plagued again by psychosomatic problems. Thinking of John, my whole left side goes numb and stays that way for a week. I am scared but won't see a doctor. Michael is as depressed about John as I am. He doesn't want to talk about the hopelessness of John's condition. He gets antsy when I bring it up. He doesn't know the answer to my endless "what will happen to him?" questions. Michael's immune system is taxed from the stress and worry and when he gets a terrible flu he moves into the guest bedroom to sleep. When his flu gets better he continues to sleep there. "I can't stand that radio of yours going off in the middle of the night," he says. Things grow tense between us. I try to lure him back to the bedroom with promises of the radio being so low he can't hear it, and how I will put crisp sheets on the beds every other day. Nothing works. I go to bed alone in the big master bedroom.

Like Beaver Cleaver, Michael has filled the guest room with guy stuff: gun magazines, horse books, and sneakers, and it is apparent to me that he is planning to stay there for quite a while.

Michael has supported my becoming an EMT and now it is backfiring. He resents the intrusion of other people's emergencies into our private life and I am not enjoying the calls anymore. I am burning out, just as I was told I would, but of course I never believed it would happen to me.

I have fallen into the habit of bitching about everything and everyone. I am no longer cheerful. When I do go to calls I am angry with patients who are not deathly ill. "Why can't they just get a friend to drive them to the hospital?" I gripe, and I equally dislike the ones that are truly ill because they stress me out and remind me of John lying in his hospital bed.

When you expect the worst of people, you get it. In the next few months I shuttle between home and Tom Knox's office spewing my dissatisfaction. When the tone goes off I am confronted with one nasty situation after another.

A woman motorcyclist crashes her bike at the intersection in Georgetown. Her skull is cracked and she is a high-priority transport. I work on her like crazy, keeping her calm as she comes in and out of consciousness in the back of the ambulance. I know her and her husband from around town. The day after her accident I see him shopping at the grocery store and ask him how she is. He appears grateful, but says, "The wife and I were just delighted that you ambulance people didn't steal her watch." I am speechless at his insensitivity.

I get the dreaded Mrs. Gernig in the back of the rig. At eighty years old, Mrs. Gernig is a sneaky drunk and a nasty one at that. She would drink and then fall off her chair and push the pendant around her neck to alert 911. There is nothing wrong with her but she still wants to be transported to the hospital. She is what EMTs call a "frequent flyer." She wants a fuss made over her and wants the ride to the hospital. Mrs. Gernig stinks of liquor so badly that if there were an open flame in the ambulance, she and I would combust.

In gathering information for the run form I try to be discreet and ask her if she has had "a cocktail," for which she reams me out royally, making me feel that I will be sued for defamation of character if I don't immediately shut up.

Bad karma draws bad karma. I miss all the interesting calls. Tom Knox has made me promise I will not hide out at home. The question is why I bother to go at all. I miss the calls for rosy-cheeked babies who need to have their little button noses wiped, and the grateful handsome folks who send checks to the firehouse after we transport them. Instead I get the eighty-five-year-old man who has been sitting on his couch naked watching TV when he accidentally makes a BM and then moves to another chair, where he sits on his sleeping cat and calls 911. I spend the better part of the next hour picking cat hair out of this old man's ass crack. I get the calls for the demented spinster sisters who live in a ramshackle house by the railroad tracks with their books and high-falutin' college degrees framed on the wall. They speak in cultured accents as they recline on sofas reeking of their urine.

Michael is still holed up in the guest room. Nothing is going right; even my uniform is driving me crazy. The jumpsuit that I wear to night calls has shrunk in the dryer to the point that when I sit down the pants end about twelve inches above my ankles. I look like I am wearing capri pants as I trudge into the hospital pushing someone on a stretcher.

I start to develop a tremor. I hope it is nerves but I fear it is Parkinson's disease. I talk to Tom Knox, who sends me to a neurologist. He assures me that it is a benign condition. However, I am so trembly that when I wrap the blood pressure cuff around a patient's arm, my hands shake so badly that the cuff falls off. When I am stressed, which is now all the time, I look like I am having a palsied fit. If I were a patient I would not allow me to touch me.

"There are three ways to treat the tremor," Tom says. "First, cut out caffeine." As he talks, I look at the row of take-out cups of Starbuck's coffee on his desk. Tom is legendary at the Starbuck's near his office because he drinks his coffee with six shots of espresso. I drink one measly cup of coffee a day and am not about to give it up. "Or you can take a beta-blocker," Tom says. "It will stop the tremors and might lessen your adrenaline rush in situations where you feel panicky."

I like the sound of this and I leave the office with a prescription. Beta-blockers are used primarily for people with high blood pressure. They regulate the heartbeat and keep blood pressure from shooting up. But they are also used for stagefright and other conditions where nerves take over and render the person unable to cope. I am wildly excited about finding a drug that will keep me from shaking and also cure my panic attacks. I stop at the drugstore and fill the prescription on the way home, so eager to try it I pop a pill on the spot.

As soon as I get home the ambulance tone goes off. I jump in the car and drive fast to the house of Stephen Demeter, one of Georgetown's most highly regarded citizens. Mr. and Mrs. Demeter are in their eighties, both playwrights and part of the original small group of creative people who found their way to rural Connecticut fifty years ago. They are town legends, they live on a gracious farm, their house overflows with art, and sunshine streams in their studio windows.

Bernice is excited about the call. "Maybe they will invite us back for tea next week," she says.

The call isn't a terrible medical crisis. Mr. Demeter is having trouble with his legs and his home care aide thinks it best he go to the hospital. As we load him into the ambulance, I admire his patrician profile; this man is still handsome at eighty-three. I also notice that I feel extremely odd, as if I don't have enough blood in my body, numb and spacey and on the verge of being very dizzy as I climb in the back of the rig. Bernice chats with Mr. Demeter as she takes vitals. I start to copy them down on the notepad, but feel like my body is wooden. About seven minutes into the twenty-minute ride to the hospital I am overcome with a huge wave of nausea and dizziness. I have the urge to lie flat; I feel like I will pass out if I don't. I try to keep it to myself, but with each curve and bump the ambulance takes I feel worse, as if all the blood is draining from my brain. I fight the feeling as best I can and when I can fight it no more I sort of slump onto the side bench in the ambulance that we use to transport a second patient. I lie in this slumped position, trying to not pass out, praying that we will get to the hospital soon. Bernice gives me a concerned look. She has no idea why I have crumpled into a fetal position.

It's an odd thing to be sick in the back of the ambulance when you are not the patient. All I want to do is push Mr. Demeter off the stretcher and climb onto the white-sheeted bed. I also want to not be going to the hospital. I know we are heading to a place filled with doctors and nurses but I just want to go home and crawl into my own bed and be left in peace. I am afraid of being sick, of being powerless.

We unload Mr. Demeter at the ER and I run into the washroom. My face is paste-colored, my collar ringed with sweat. I am pissed off at myself. "Now what's wrong with you, you asshole?" I say into the mirror at my ghostly reflection. I stagger back outside. Bernice is handing the nurse Mr. Demeter's chart. "I'm not feeling so well," I mumble. "I think I'll go outside and get some air."

The ride back to the firehouse seems endless. Bernice takes my blood pressure, or she attempts to. It has plunged so low that she has trouble finding it at all. "I took a pill," I say, trailing off weakly, waving my free hand about like a Victorian lady with a case of the vapors.

Back at the firehouse I leave her with the paperwork and run toward my car. By the time I pull into the garage I am ready to crash. What to do, call 911? Take another ride in the ambulance that I just got out of? I think not.

I call Tom Knox's emergency number. He calls me right back. "You are highly sensitive to beta-blockers," he says calmly. "You will feel better in the morning." I crawl into bed. It takes four days before I feel normal. I am now totally phobic about riding in the ambulance again.

I am back at Tom Knox's office, back at square one. I hold out a shaking hand. "See," I say, and my hand twitches.

"It's called benign essential tremor," Tom says, seconding the opinion of the neurologist.

"I look like a spastic," I say. "What else can I do beside take beta-blockers?"

"Liquor will stop the tremors, as will Valium." He smiles. "Of course, don't use them together, and obviously you can't drink before going on a call."

I want to test the theory, so when I leave his office I head to the liquor store, where I buy a bottle of gin, a bottle of bourbon, and a bottle of scotch. I come home and unload my haul in the kitchen.

"What's that for?" Michael asks. He hasn't seen me drink since he went on the wagon two years ago. I stopped drinking as a show of support.

"Me," I answer. "I am going to get drunk so I can be an EMT again."

"Huh?" Michael says. I ignore him as I pour three shots of Maker's Mark and some ginger ale into a tall glass, add ice, and stir. I walk to my favorite chair and sit down. I am not much of a drinker. Booze was never a big deal to me; it was easy to put it aside, and I thought Michael would enjoy it if when I went to a restaurant with him I didn't order my ubiquitous whiskey sour.

I forgot that I like the taste of this drink and swill it down fast.

As a science experiment I hold up my left hand and watch it shake. I watch it carefully to see if when the liquor hits my brain it stops shaking. I sit there for maybe ten minutes. I think I am seeing less of a tremor, but I am also seeing two hands where there was one. I am suddenly startlingly drunk. I get up to go to the bathroom and I lurch, I trip over Clementine, my brindle bullmastiff, who rolls out of the way. I look at her face and begin to laugh. She looks just like the Cookie Puss Carvel Cake: a big flat face with chocolate saucer eyes. I feel better than I did with the beta-blocker; in fact, I feel great in a soused, shit-faced kind of way. But there is no way I could go on an EMT call like this. I hit the speed dial and get Tom Knox's message on the phone.

"I had a drink," I half belch. "I'm not so shaky as I was but I'm too drunk to talk." I hang up.

I sit stupefied in front of the TV watching an infomercial for George Foreman's grilling machine. I need one, right now. I am going to call the 800 number but am too woozy to get my Visa card and bother with it. I sit there and watch George making steaks and watching the fat drain out. "So healthful," I think. I am mesmerized by George's shiny brown head. Eventually I get bored and stagger up to bed and sleep it off.

18

I need something to break the spell of the bad stuff. All I think about is John's stroke and my own mental problems. I need something that will bring me back in sync with the joy of the firehouse and being an EMT.

I became an EMT because it was a way to get out of my own depressed head, and think about other people's problems, but it seems I have become immune to the antidote. I am back wallowing in my mental mess.

Things between Michael and me are strained and getting worse. We have been married thirty-three years and are acting like we don't know each other. In an attempt to heal what appears to be broken we start marriage therapy. We meet once a week with a woman therapist who is thoughtful and kind, yet at the end of each session I want to run screaming into oncoming traffic. Michael and I find fault with each other. We nitpick and criticize. We drag up wrongs and misdeeds from decades past. We finger-point and accuse, we become amnesiac about what we possibly could have seen in each other. It is beyond excruciating to sit in the therapist's office each week and tell each other how we feel the other one has failed us. We are too angry to stop bitching and too much in love to leave the marriage.

Our therapy sessions are on Wednesdays and I spend all week dreading the pain that I know will be there. It is like root canal of the heart. I love Michael; he says he loves me. But we don't like each other at all. Our many books written together are like our children; we can't leave the marriage because of them. We have more books together in us. I can't write them being just friends with Michael. I have to be in love and be loved for the words to flow.

But the words that are flowing between us are still critical and angry. "You said . . . You did . . . Why did you look at her . . . What did you mean by . . ."

With each business trip we take for *Gourmet* and each column we write together, the tension grows. I cannot get through an hour of driving in the car or pulling into a motel room without tears flowing down my face. Michael drives and I cry. I cry my way through Iowa and Michigan and Texas. I cry every time I see couples our age together, I cry when I see anniversary cakes in the windows of small-town bakeries, I cry when I am in bed at night and look at Michael's sleeping profile and wonder if this is *fini*.

When I am at home I am crying too. I am on the phone with Tom Knox daily. He is guiding me through the couples therapy. He doesn't know what the outcome will be. I keep pushing him to tell me a "they lived happily ever after" ending, but he won't. When I come into his office he looks serious and I go through half a box of Kleenex. My best friend, Bunny, calls three times a day to check on me. I am often in bed, sleeping. She recommends books to read and faxes me meditations on relationships. They make me cry more, but I am so glad for her friendship. I have become a pathetic case. I go to Bernice's house and sit at her dining table and cry as I drink the coffee she makes me, I call another dear friend, Joanne, who is like a mother to me, and weep for hours, until my ear turns red from holding the phone to it.

Michael and I have business commitments to fulfill and a mortgage to pay so we plow on as best we can. One of our commitments is a monthly column for *Connecticut Magazine,* in which we find stores around the state that sell unusual things, and write about them.

We are heading this morning to Bridgeport. We have found a store that sells clerical robes to the clergy and stocks a cleaner that gets sacramental wine stains out of carpets.

The morning has started badly already. We fight as soon as we wake up. I have not a clue what we were fighting about and I suspect Michael doesn't either. It is just more of the blame and guilt and needs-unmet conundrum that we have unleashed on each other since we began seeing the marriage therapist. It is like a badminton game from hell, each of us walloping the frail bird across the net, *whoop,* as hard as we can.

We are five minutes from the religious store and my face is tearstained. I feel dry heaves coming on. Michael looks stony-faced as he drives. I dry my tears on an old paper towel crumpled in my purse and spray Binaca in my mouth. I take a long, slow breath and try to center myself. We park in front of the store. My head is reeling and I cannot shut my mouth, although I know I should. I keep upping the ante to get Michael to feel the pain I am in. "I just want you to know," I say, hiccuping with grief, "I called the suicide hotline yesterday."

Michael glowers at me. "Are you telling me you want to kill yourself?" he asks. His light blue eyes look like bits of an Arctic glacier to me. I have no idea what the answer is. "I do, I don't, I don't know . . . I can't live without you," I stammer. This has backfired on me. Instead of taking me in his arms, I have alienated Michael even more with my raging codependency. We are back at square one, and I try my best to compose myself as I walk into the religious store.

I am surrounded by icons and portraits of Jesus and the Virgin Mary. Not being a Christian, I feel oddly embarrassed to be there; I feel that I am looking at what is for sale with an ironic, slightly kitsch attitude. I wish I were religious, part of an organized faith whose rituals I could cling to as I pass through this hard period with Michael. I envy the rosaries and the statuettes and the holy cards. I do know that if I were a Catholic I would be as big a spanker as I am as an EMT; I would have one of everything, I would have the biggest, shiniest cross in the store and an illuminated Jesus on my dashboard.

Michael and I walk around the store and I start to notice that the small staff of three are huddled around a radio, that our entrance seems to have gone unnoticed. We walk up to them and they scarcely acknowledge our presence. They look gray-faced and frozen in place. One of them tells us, "A plane . . . it just hit the World Trade Tower." My hand goes to my mouth. I imagine a tiny Piper Cub, off its route, smashing like a mosquito into the unyielding building. Michael and I stop talking and listen to the radio with them. What we hear is frankly unbelievable. It is not a tiny plane but a 767, and now, wait, another jet has hit the second tower and the buildings are falling, collapsing like a crazy wedding cake, tier after tier, into themselves. The religious store staff is too stunned to talk, the voice from the radio pierces the air. Michael and I look at each other. I start to shake with fear. I am too scared to cry. We run to our car parked outside and start the engine. We turn on the radio and listen to the news. "Oh my God," we both say. I grab Michael's arm and squeeze it hard. This has got to be a practical joke, like Orson Welles's "War of the Worlds" broadcast.

It is now 11 A.M., and we have driven home from Bridgeport to our house at top speed. We run to the TV, the Twin Towers' collapse remains unreal until we see it. And then we see it, over and over, a hideous loop, the buildings falling and then falling again. People screaming and running, the streets gray with ashes, the sky black with smoke billowing like in the Apocalypse. I look away from the TV and at Michael. I feel like I haven't seen him in years. I see him without the anger and pain and tears that have come between. He is just Michael and I am just Jane and we live together in a yellow house on a hill, and we love each other. It is all so simple. I bury myself in his arms and we hold each other, waiting together for the world to end.

I hug Michael and he hugs me back. We have no words to say to each other except that what is happening in lower Manhattan has dwarfed everything we have been mad about with each other. We are alive, the end of the world might be coming, and we are together, as we should be.

Michael and I look at each other again and again. We can hear each other's breath coming in harsh short gasps. "I love you," I say as if it might be my last words.

After a half hour of watching the TV coverage I look at my wall calendar: 9/11. How ironic: 911. That is me, I remember. I do a strange thing. I run upstairs to my bedroom and pull out my EMT full dress uniform. I have never worn it, so it sits wrapped in tissue paper in a plastic bin at the bottom of the closet. I pull off my jeans and T-shirt and fling them on the floor. Then I get dressed. First the blue uniform shirt with the American flag patch sewed on one sleeve, the Georgetown Fire Department shield on the other. Next come the uniform pants, navy blue with a gold cord up the side. I belt the pants on, and then add the navy blue tie, shiny laced black shoes, and a fireman's dress hat with a silver badge pinned on it. I place my white dress gloves in the shirt's epaulets.

I run down to the den where the TV set is. Michael looks at me, and then does a double take. I am dressed to be buried at Arlington National Cemetery. I am too freaked out to sit down, so I watch television standing at attention, crying and blowing my nose in a paper towel from the kitchen. Every time I see a flag or a policeman or an EMT on the TV, I salute.

In chaos we each do what we can. I stand in full dress uniform in front of the TV with an ear to my police radio, waiting to be called. I will die like a soldier with my boots on. The Twin Towers have fallen and then we hear about the plane hitting the Pentagon and I wonder if the little oxygen tank, rolls of bandages, and oral airways I have in the back of my car will be of any use if a plane crashes in the middle of Georgetown.

I stand guarding the police radio. Michael reacts in his own odd way. He jumps in the car, drives to the service station and fills it with gas, then goes to the grocery store and buys a dozen steaks, some bottled water, and many cans of dog food. When he comes home the steaks go in the refrigerator and Michael runs upstairs to his office, where he pulls a selection of guns from his closet. He takes out a Kalashnikov assault rifle, an evil-looking weapon, one of the many guns he has collected over the years. He loads bullets into magazines and lays the magazines in a neat line on his desk.

We are each facing the end of the world in our own way. I am going down in uniform. Michael will eat steaks and shoot the enemy and, oh, yes, feed the dog. I would say we are insane, but so is the world at the moment.

Hours pass. I can't believe I have not been toned out yet. Finally I sit down; I am no longer capable of standing at attention. My feet and knees hurt. I feel very old and very tired. I go upstairs and change clothes.

"Let's go to Heibeck's and fill up the other car with gas," Michael says.

We jump in our blue Dodge SUV and drive the two miles from our house to the gas station. After we pump the gas we walk into the little office where the Heibeck brothers are watching the news on TV. I see the chief standing, looking up at the screen. His face is ashen. I think I see his eyes tearing. The Heibeck brothers and I look at each other, we shake our heads. There is really nothing to say. Michael and I drive home with a tank full of gas, waiting vigilantly.

We sleep deeply and exhaustedly. By the next morning my tone has still not gone off. I have taken off my dress uniform and put on a navy blue jumpsuit with EMS written on the back. I have slept in it. All the steaks are still in the refrigerator, as Michael and I are too nauseous to eat. I have made only one phone call, to Bernice, whom I reach on her cell phone. She is in her car driving to

Boston to see her parents. "Please come home," I say. "I need you to be here for calls." Fortunately, she has already decided to return to Georgetown.

It seems like half the world is driving into New York City. Fire departments and EMS squads are on their way from all over the country. Georgetown is only an hour and a half away from the city. We wait for the chief to tell us what to do. Other EMS units from our area have been dispatched. We finally get the command: we are not going to Ground Zero; we are to stay in Georgetown to care for the people of the town. I am both disappointed and relieved. Frankly, I am scared to death to go to Ground Zero. I don't know if I can take it emotionally or physically. I don't have much time to ponder this decision because suddenly the tones go off, and keep going off. I go to calls all day and all night. It is as if the community had collectively held its breath the day the planes flew into the towers, but now everyone is reacting all at once. We go out on one 911 call after another. People are fainting, having chest pains, panic attacks, symptoms of strokes. Because Georgetown is so close to New York City, many people had family members or friends who were killed in the collapse of the towers. All the churches and the synagogues open their doors to the public. If you drive by with your car windows open you can hear organ music and crying.

We are so near to New York and yet so far. It would take an hour and fifteen minutes to get from the firehouse to the remains of the Twin Towers. But we don't go. It is a wise and selfless decision; there are more than enough rescue crews there, and we are needed in our small town.

I am exhausted from taking people to the local hospital, but I am now too edgy to go to bed. In my EMT jacket and in my well-labeled EMT car I cruise the town when the sun goes down. Silently, like a bat, like a stealth bomber, I am looking for terrorists, I am looking for victims.

The Monday night after the attacks we have our regular firehouse meeting. I walk upstairs and see everyone watching the news on TV. They look grim.

Bin Laden's face is on the TV. "Kill him" is murmured in unison. I see the firemen clench their fists. If he were in Georgetown, he wouldn't stand a chance.

We start to have drills about what to do if terrorism strikes close to home. We are issued big white biohazard suits and learn how to put them on. We learn how to wash people down who have been exposed to anthrax. We learn how to decontaminate ourselves. We go over incident command systems. We view photographs of the municipal buildings around Georgetown, the reservoirs, and other likely terrorist targets.

Suddenly being an EMT is much more than I bargained for. My self-centered fears and small victories are dwarfed by the Twin Towers, on fire and crumbling like the scariest of tarot cards: the Tower. Countless firemen and EMS workers have been killed doing their job. Others work around the clock, digging out, looking for survivors. I feel tiny by comparison to this unspeakable effort. Georgetown feels tiny too. We are one little star in a huge galaxy of rescue workers. I am connected with the people at Ground Zero, yet light-years away. I am but one of many. One of a brotherhood of thousands of rescue workers. It doesn't matter if my hands shake or my pants are too short, I am still one of them.

19

Becoming an EMT has allowed me to do the impossible. I am thinking of how true this is as I am sitting behind the wheel of one of Georgetown's fire trucks.

Bernice has decided that she has to get a 2Q driver's license. This legally allows the operator to drive vehicles over 26,000 pounds, huge vehicles like fire trucks. Jimmy Mecozzi, a professional fireman in Stratford, Connecticut, and a longtime member of the Georgetown Volunteer Fire Department, is the instructor. Bernice has lured me into taking the class. The idea of driving a fire truck seems so silly to me, an ex–New Yorker who didn't know how to drive a car until I was twenty-three, that I said, "Sure, why not," in a moment of unbridled lunacy.

Bernice and I report to the parking lot of the local high school on a Sunday. The lot is empty, except for our few empty parked cars, and Jimmy Mecozzi and the big red fire engine. Bernice steps out of her Lexus and a smile immediately stretches my face. She is wearing shorts, her legs are trim and tanned, and on her head is a large straw hat covered with silk flowers.

We are not the only people who have signed up for the course. There are a number of young men from the fire department who also want to be trained. We are issued a yellow manual from the Connecticut Fire Academy. I thumb through it and the smile that started with Bernice's flowered hat has now turned to outright laughter. I might as well have been given a manual for decoding a Martian spaceship. I recognize nothing at all familiar. There are diagrams of push rods and cam rollers, manual draining valves and slack adjusters. I see Jimmy Mecozzi looking at me as I laugh like a loon. His face lights up happily. I suspect he thinks I am digging the heavy-metalness of it all. Everyone at the firehouse loves Jimmy Mecozzi. The Mecozzis have been active members of the firehouse forever. Jimmy used to be a volunteer fireman and now is a professional. He is tall and handsome and has a disarming grin. He tells great stories about fighting fires in Bridgeport and Stratford. He always has a skin-crawling tale about finding a cadaver dead so long, its face fell off when it was moved, or zillions of rats leaping out from behind walls that the firemen chopped down. He brings in his fireman's hat that has recently melted into a burned wad from a flashback fire. He shows it off to all the young firemen as a cautionary tale.

I explain to Jimmy why I am taking the 2Q class. It

goes something like this: "If there were no firemen left on earth and the truck absolutely *had* to get to a fire, then I would drive it."

"It's good for everyone to know how to drive the apparatus," he says. "You'll do fine."

We all stand around dwarfed by the huge shiny truck. It really is a gorgeous thing. I love the gold lettering on the side that says GEORGETOWN. We are going to do a walk-around. I wonder if this is like a walkabout, recalling a Crocodile Dundee movie that had Aborigines doing this on a regular basis in order to go into a mystical trance. I find there is nothing transcendental about walking around the fire truck. It reminds me of what you see people do when they buy a used car. You basically walk around tapping things and peeking at them from below. Jimmy tells us, "You will check the manual slack adjusters on the S cam brakes. Use gloves and pull hard on each slack adjuster that you can get to, check the brake drums and the linings; they must not have cracks longer than one-half the width of the friction area."

I have been in 2Q class twenty minutes and I am already totally lost. I walk around the truck banging on things, pulling things, and squatting down under it to pretend to look at stuff. Jimmy finds all sorts of things in need of repair on the truck. He shows them to us, but nothing registers with me. I shake my head yes as if I get it. When I get tense I look at Bernice's petunia-ridden hat, which cheers me up.

By the second hour of this first class the students are

allowed to climb up into the cab and get the feel of what it is like behind the wheel. We hit the right switches and the ignition goes on. The steering wheel is huge and flat, not in an upright position like a car. Climbing up into the cab has taken effort, I am already breathing hard. Jimmy sits in the passenger seat. I am the driver. He has placed orange cones around the parking lot, and he expects that we will all drive forward slowly, and then around the obstacle course. With the ignition on, I grab the wheel in a death grip. This truck is huge. It weighs 45,000 pounds and is twenty-seven feet long. Jimmy Mecozzi puts his seat belt on, which I think is a mighty good idea. He coaches me to step on the gas pedal and make the truck move forward. My toe taps it so gently that nothing happens. I am exerting so little force I would not break a spiderweb. He keeps encouraging me, and finally I depress the petal enough so the truck moves. I instantly hit the brake, lurching us to a stop. "That's good," Jimmy says optimistically. "Now you see that the brakes work. Let's go forward again." After half an hour I have summoned up enough nerve to actually drive the truck, albeit very slowly, around the orange cones. I am probably going ten miles an hour but I feel like an unstoppable juggernaut. I am looking in both side mirrors and all I see is endless yards of truck behind me. "Now slow down and stop," Jimmy says, and when I hit the brakes it feels like nothing is happening. The truck is so much heavier than a car that even going ten miles an hour, it seems to take forever to stop.

Over the next few weeks Bernice and I take our 2Q lessons together. She is a natural; in her shorts and sandals, with brightly painted toenails, she drives the truck forward, backward, and around the cones, stops smoothly, and climbs out of the cab with ease. I love taking the lessons but it is clear to me from the beginning that I have some sort of spatial dyslexia. When Jimmy says go right, I go left. I run over the orange cones. When I back up I come dangerously close to the brick wall of the high school. Over the roar of the engine I hear people on the ground yelling, "*Stop!*" Michael comes by the parking lot one Saturday morning with a camera and takes pictures of me and Bernice in front of the truck. I have a feeling I will not see the end of the 2Q class, so I want something for posterity.

Bernice and I arrange a special practice session with Jimmy Mecozzi late one afternoon. We are actually going to drive the fire truck on the road. Bernice goes first. She and Jimmy are gone at least half an hour. She has a triumphant look on her face when they return. The sun has gone down and it is now dark. I am absolutely terrified of driving the truck at night. I can't see where I am going during the day, and now it is all shadows and darkness.

"Just relax," Jimmy says as he sees my white knuckles around the wheel. I'm chewing my gum hard, because I need some saliva. With Jimmy's encouragement, I slowly pull the truck out of the firehouse bay. I bite my lower lip as I see how close the side mirrors are to the garage door.

"Okay now, when we get out on the road we are going to go right and turn right again on Route 57." I creep slowly along the road, so slowly the speedometer hardly moves. "You can pick up the pace now," Jimmy says. I gingerly press the gas pedal harder. I feel the truck pick up speed. I make a decent turn and we are going down Route 57, which at this hour is blessedly empty. I get the truck up to about twenty miles an hour, which feels superfast. I can feel a nice breeze blowing in the open windows of the truck. "Faster," Jimmy says, and again I press the pedal closer to the floor. We are a few miles from the firehouse and I am now going about forty. The blood has rushed back into my hands as I have relaxed my grasp. "Turn here," Jimmy says. I take my eyes off the road for a moment and look at him. He is really handsome. I can see why when his name is mentioned by the ladies of the firehouse it is followed by a sigh. We head down one road, and then another, I am taking the curves with authority. Cars pull over when I pass them. We reach the big senior citizen housing development in the process of being built in Georgetown. It is still under construction, and no one is around at night. "Park at the bottom of the driveway," Jimmy instructs, and I manage to get in the right position. "Now," he says with a big grin, "I want you to drive the truck backward up the driveway."

I know this driveway; I have driven it during the day, forward, in my Subaru. It is serpentine and narrow. "You have to be kidding," I say to him.

"You can do it," he says, and I see a flicker in his eyes

that explains to me why firemen are a breed apart from the rest of us. He has absolutely no fear. He sees no reason why I, who can't tell right from left, shouldn't back up a half-mile-long driveway with ruts on either side in the dark in an immense fire truck. I breathe in his courage. I relax my hands and look at the mirrors on each side of the truck. Everything is backward, everything looks closer or farther than it really is. I slip the gears into reverse and start to hit the gas pedal. I can hardly see the road and the ditches are obscured by shadows. I look at Jimmy, who looks calm and amused. "C'mon," he says, "it's easy."

I have a choice. I can sit in the cab next to this handsome fireman and tell him the long sad story of my life, all the childhood abuse I have suffered, my recurring depressions, the strength of my Prozac prescription, all my fears and anxieties, or I can just do it. I choose the latter. I clear my mind of its racing thoughts; I exist only in this moment. I have no history at all. It is up to me to stay put or go forward (or in this case backward) and before I can overthink what to do and the hundred reasons why I can't, I am doing it. Backing up the driveway at a fast clip, spinning the steering wheel, watching how I am able to keep the giant tires out of the ruts on either side of the unfinished driveway.

"Good job!!!" Jimmy says. I go at a quick pace down the driveway. I know my way back to the firehouse. Jimmy jumps out when we get there and guides me and the truck back into the bay.

"Thanks," I say to him, as we close the bay door and head for our cars.

"That was good," Jimmy says. I smile at him. I smile my big smile, which shows the crack on my front tooth at the gum line that I am self-conscious about. I smell sweaty, but that's okay too. I keep smiling all the way home. I dream about the fire truck that night, I dream that I am at the wheel and that Jimmy Mecozzi and I are driving eighty miles an hour through the wheat fields of Nebraska. It is flat as a plate and we are the only vehicle on the road.

I wake up having never felt so purely happy. When the state instructor shows up a month later to give the 2Q test, Bernice passes. I do not show up for the test. I don't know why I chose to stay home, but I think I felt that my ability to drive the fire truck that night was like a fairy tale; that in the bright plebeian light of day, the magic would be gone, and I would again not know my right from my left. I do not want to see my fairy coach turn into a pumpkin.

20

It has been more than two years since I became an EMT at Georgetown. I have been there long enough to have to recertify, so I must take refresher courses in everything I know, hit the books again, show instructors that I can use the defibrillator correctly, do CPR, insert an oral airway correctly. The recertification class is much more homey than the class I originally took in New Canaan. There are about eight of us, and we are all EMTs already, so we are treated with respect by paramedic Harry Downs, who teaches the class. It is fun. Our chief, Mike Heibeck, and our assistant chief, his brother Marty, are in the class, as is Charlie Pfhal, whom I have come to adore. It is hard for me to remember how scared I was of him when he first showed me the ambulance; now when we see each other we give each other a big hug. Dot is there, too. It feels like old times when she comes in to each class slightly late, throws her backpack down on the desk, and scowls at everyone. I realize how much a part of it all she is.

In recert class, which runs about four hours a night over the course of eight weeks, we take a break in the middle of the class. Someone runs out for pizzas or a six-foot hero sandwich from the local grocery store. We gobble it down with cans of Pepsi from the soda machine.

I like being at the firehouse for recert class; I feel truly safe here. I like that things stay the same, that life is logical and predictable. The meetings and drills happen on schedule. The big TV in the great room is still tuned to NASCAR races, notices for parades we can march in are posted on the bulletin board. Even the things that change happen slowly, at a pace I can digest.

We get a new ambulance. It is a state-of-the art, glorious vehicle. We meet as a committee to choose all the details. The guys choose the chassis and engine and the girls choose the color scheme. It's a sexist cliché, but that is how we do it. Bernice and I have our hearts set on a soothing blue interior. Bernice wants to add glue-on glow-in-the-dark stars on the ceiling so the patients will have something nice to look at.

Some people find the monthly meetings and drills boring. I adore them. It is what my family never did: sit down together and talk about things, even argue safely (the firehouse president bangs his gavel if things get out of hand). Everything from a new dishwasher to painting the stairwell is debated and discussed. People get hot under the collar but it still seems safe. The chief, the president, and the firehouse secretary, who all sit at the big table in the front of the room, are in control. I can relax here.

I love the meetings. I love standing at attention and saying the Pledge of Allegiance. I love hearing the minutes of the last meeting. I love how the secretary, Greg Zap, reads the correspondence at the end of the meetings, notes and letters from people in Georgetown who thank us for our help. Most people outside the firehouse don't understand how meaningful these notes are to us.

After the meeting I follow the crowd back to the TV room, where I join in the ritual of eating hard-boiled eggs, M&M's, and cookies. I look around and feel a great swell of comfort wash over me. Like Ralph Cramden at his Raccoon Lodge, this is my special place.

Charlie Pfhal walks toward me. He often comes over to talk after a meeting; sometimes he asks me for a recipe for his wife, to whom he has been married for fifty years. He had been in an officers' meeting that took place before the general monthly meeting. "Young lady," he says (this is what he calls me), "we were wondering if you would take over the role of firehouse secretary when Greg Zap's term is over."

I am agog. The role of secretary means that at the monthly meetings I get to sit at the big table with the top three, my name on the list of people in command not far below those of the chief and the president.

"Yes, absolutely," I stammer, thinking maybe I have heard him wrong.

But I haven't, and over the next month I am shown the file cabinet where the monthly meeting minutes go back decades. The original ones are old and yellowed with age, handwritten and to the point. I plunge my hand in and bring out 1949. I see Eddie's name, as a member of a "card committee." Eddie is the man who stopped coming to the meetings last year when he couldn't smoke his cigar in the firehouse anymore. There is an accounting of $2.81 cents paid to Heibeck's Garage, a memo that a motion was made and seconded to buy two "books of chances" from the Riverside Fire Department, someone gave a donation of $10.00 to the ambulance, and a motion was made to buy a wheelchair for the firehouse, as well as rent a tank of oxygen at a cost of $1.00 per year.

There have only been five firehouse secretaries since the firehouse began. Oddly enough, one of them—a retired member who has since moved away—is the man who built and sold the house Michael and I live in now, and Charlie Pfhal did all the interior painting and wallpapering in our house back in the 1950s.

It is finally time for me to take over as secretary. I am given a special set of keys that opens the chief's office door (where the secretary's file cabinet is kept), a special license plate for the front of my car (ahhh, bliss), and an attaché case that, like my front license plate, has a thick sign that says SECRETARY, FIRE DEPT., GEORGETOWN, CT. screwed onto its side. The case is a vintage American Tourister, pebbly black with a red interior, and looks like it is from the early 1960s. Inside the case is a mix of wonderful things, blank greeting cards for "Get Well" or "Sympathy," meeting minutes, financial reports, and manila envelopes filled with names and phone numbers so I can call or send fruit baskets to members who are sick.

Greg Zap walks over to me, and in a heartfelt way hands me the briefcase. We smile at each other because it seems sort of corny but we both know it is an important moment. He is handing me the history of the Georgetown Fire Company from its inception. I will be the first woman secretary. I open the briefcase when I get home. Greg has left me a gift inside. Three inexpensive Evermore cigars, made in Connecticut, in a small white cigar box. These are what he smokes. I never smoke them but I keep the box of cigars in the briefcase forever. I am now "one of the boys." Along with the cigars comes a gift from Tom Pasiuk, a very quiet man who has been a firehouse member for over twenty-five years. "My friend made this and I thought you would like it," he says, and hands me a pair of small wooden pinchers. I have absolutely no idea what they do. "I figured a lady like you would need toast tongs," he says shyly. I imagine myself in his eyes being like Mrs.Toplofty, a character in the old Emily Post etiquette books, who always knew the correct fork to use. The toast tongs go in the briefcase with the cigars.

The first monthly meeting comes, and there is an empty chair for me at the big table in the front of the room. The chief nods at me, the president bangs his gavel, and we all stand for the Pledge of Allegiance. I place my right hand on my heart and face the flag; ". . . one nation, under God, indivisible . . ." I say along with the rest. *Indivisible.* I think of what that word means: united, one of a group of many, not alone. When I was a kid I thought the word was *invisible,* which is how I felt most of the time. I sit down at the front table and thirty-two people look at me. They see me, I am real, I am here, and I am part of something, at last.

ambulance girl

Jane Stern

Questions for discussion:

1. Stern seems to find the experience of anonymity refreshing, even euphoric. Of her first day in a hospital emergency room, she writes, "I am just a spare pair of hands that day. I have no name, no authority...I am hooked." Similarly, her strategy for getting through the terrifying experience of driving a fire truck for the first time is to tell herself, "I exist only in this moment. I have no history at all." Why is this displacement of self so attractive to her? Do you see it as a form of denial or as a healthy—perhaps even necessary—release from self-absorption?

2. Stern's encounter with her "first dead guy" drives home the inevitability of unanswerable questions in life. She wants to know why the man's brother didn't notice he was blue, why the brother suffers from a grotesque facial deformity, why the brother failed to call 911 earlier in the day. How does she deal with these questions? Do we identify with her reactions?

3. Why does Stern call duct tape "the operative semantic symbol of the dividing line between Fairfield County snooty and Fairfield County down-to-earth"? How does the disparity between New Canaan—where Stern takes her EMT training and "where the ambulance cot blankets look like the monogrammed coverings of show horses"—and Georgetown mirror the dispar-

ity between Stern's pre-EMT and post-EMT lives? How do Stern's friends react to her sudden decision to become an EMT?

4. How does Stern's induction into the EMT world alter her perception of her hometown? Why does she note that "now when I stop at the service station my eyes are cast downward with humility"?

5. Stern's moment of reckoning comes on a grounded airplane, where she is trapped for six hours with no food, no fresh air, and a clogged toilet. Discuss her statement, "I died the thousand deaths of a coward before the plane finally took off." What allows her to recall in retrospect the one moment on the plane when she "didn't feel like the whole world was collapsing"? How do you think Stern would react to being trapped for six hours on a grounded plane today?

6. The class about head injuries throws Stern completely off balance. What painful family memories does the session dredge up, and why does she remind herself, "It is important to know that there will not be anyone waiting under the window to kill me"? What simple gesture snaps her back to reality? Why?

7. As she volunteers at the low-tech, profoundly not scary Georgetown Haunted House on Halloween, Stern contemplates a lifetime of fear. She writes, "Knowledge replaces terror for me, and instead of being afraid I can now safely watch one of the Heibeck brothers' young sons lying on a table, covered with raw

chicken livers, screaming as if he is having live surgery performed on him." In what way does this sum up the theme of Stern's memoir?

8. When John, a beloved father figure to Stern and her husband, Michael, emerges from a two-week coma, he is brain damaged, partly paralyzed, and has lost all memory of his rich life. Stern is devastated to realize that, in certain circumstances, a successful EMT "save" is perhaps no more than a crass intervention in what might be a timely death. How does this realization affect her? How does it change the EMT work she performs in the following weeks?

about the author

JANE STERN has coauthored thirty books about American culture and food with her husband, Michael Stern. Their books have appeared on the *New York Times* bestseller list. She also coauthors a monthly column for *Gourmet* magazine, which has won several James Beard Awards for writing. Jane Stern lives in Redding, Connecticut, with Michael, two horses, one dog, and one parrot.